Unfinis

The Other Side of Fame

A Mother's Story About The Loss Of Her Famous Daughter Kristen Pfaff

Janet A. Pfaff

Table of Contents

Preface

This book has been 20 years in the making. As a parent with a real life-changing experience, I want to share the story of how I lost my daughter, Kristen Pfaff, the bass guitarist in the band *Hole*, to an accidental heroin overdose in Seattle, Washington on June 15, 1994. I wish to let the reader know what she accomplished in her short life.

I will relate how her death impacted my life, as well as my family's lives. However, in no way do I intend to glorify the lifestyle or influence of the performers who set the stage for this tragedy. Her death has been difficult to accept and impossible to understand. If anything, I have a message of how God has helped, and continues to help me, through the grieving process. One aspect of this healing was to share with kids, teens, and young adults the perils of drug abuse. As a result, my journey to convey my message has taken me to places to which I would never have traveled if it was not for this experience.

My efforts have been painstaking attempts at reasoning through the trauma of her loss, not only of my precious child, but of the talent and potential that was lost to future generations. For these reasons, it is my goal that her memory will live on through this book, which reveals her true personality, literary skill, and zest for living.

In closing, consider this quote by E. K. Jones, which is engraved on the front of the Lockport (NY) Public Library: "Books are like an open door to set the spirit free." As a result of this book's publication, I hope to set Kristen's spirit free, as well as my own.

Acknowledgements

I want to thank and express my deepest gratitude and respect for those who have helped me to make this book a reality. First and foremost, my daughter, Kristen, who continuously teaches me through her short life; my son, Jason, whom I adore and am deeply grateful for; my grandson, Luke, who is an inspiration to me every day. I also appreciate my family who have supported me in many ways through these years of grieving and a very special thanks to my dear friends Kyle Dembrow, and Jeanne Turansky, whose time and heart in this project gave me the courage to forge on and move forward in the completion of a very sensitive story.

A special mention to Angela Warren, Anthony and Irene DiRaffael, Mary Cappola, the Cicciarelli Family, all the Espositos, the Kearney Family, Marcy Brimo-Walle, and thanks to God for the supernatural strength and hope that He has given to me.

Introduction

My name is Janet Pfaff and I am the mother of Kristen Pfaff, an internationally recognized female bassist, who died of a heroin overdose on June 15, 1994. She was in the rock band, *Hole*, with Courtney Love, and played on the band's major record label debut album, *Live Through This*. This album went platinum shortly after hers and Kurt Cobain's deaths, only a few months apart, in 1994. As a result, Kristen never saw the results of her efforts. I wish to dedicate this work to her. She died too soon and left heartfelt memories for those who loved her, as well as an indelible mark on the music industry. I also wish to express my disappointment in the media's failure to report the whole truth and their tendency to emphasize the sensationalism that so defines that industry. Some media insensitivity for the feelings of loved ones and family members is irreverent, to put it mildly.

This book is a series of stories and journal entries based on experiences and anecdotes that mark revelations of Kristen's short life and my journey through the grieving process. It also includes some of Kristen's writings and my insights on how I have grown and survived her death based on the passage of time. The work developed out of a journal I kept with thoughts woven throughout, resulting in a message of hope for the reader and me. In a sense, this book is written by both Kristen and me.

In telling my story, I fear that I will fall short in expressing my feelings because of my inability to totally accept, or understand, this loss. Maybe, for the time being, her memory can live on through this work which exposes her literary genius and my lack of such. However, my anguished words can only barely express the state of limbo and numbness that I have experienced and the years of silence and retreat that led to the journal which inspired me to write this book. I can only try to find some nobility for her and dignify her memory.

Chapter 1 - Prelude

In 1967 during a time of exhilaration, anti-war fever, inspired music and drama, she made her debut: a dark-haired (what there was of it), hazel-eyed, fair-skinned princess. First came the Beatles, then the Rolling Stones, now Kristen who would later become one of the country's finest female bassists. Flavored only with the times came the thunderous knock from Heaven, bringing an outburst from the clouds that hit the pre-dawn hour. No baby, just pain.

"Walk," said the doctor. "Wash the floor," said Mom. So I did all of the above.

But no baby, no water. There was thunder and lightning, but no rain. Finally on May 26, 1967, Kristen came into this world. Her father, Mike, was my first husband, whom I had married right out of high school. (My honeymoon was my first time away from home.)

Kristen at 1 year old

This was an interesting beginning for a turbulent story. I want to start with how wonderful it was to be Kristen's mother. She was such a delightful child, so self-motivated and outgoing. She had many friends. From the beginning, she was an attention getter if only for her darling appearance and endearing personality. I could never take credit for the way she turned out because she was her own person from the time she was 3 years old.

Chapter 2 - Con Spirito

During the early 1970's we lived near Santa Monica, California until the Northridge earthquake of 1971 which hit 6.9 on the Richter scale. At 6 a.m. on a cool morning, my daughter and I slept peacefully when suddenly the house began to rumble as though it were being shaken from its foundation. In the next few hours, we would experience the traumatic effects of a natural disaster. I recall that my first instinct was to flip the light switch, but to no avail. Next, I picked up the bedside phone. It was dead. My heart raced as I looked up at the ceiling and saw that it had begun to crack. Dishes spilled out of cupboards and shelves crashed to the floor as the rumbling intensified. I grabbed my little Kristen, who had slept with me, and made my way to the window. Outside, fires had erupted in the surrounding mountains and the streets were flooded. I thought it was the end of the world.

Kristen and Janet at Santa Monica Beach

As an overwhelming fear gripped me, a neighbor arrived at our door offering his assistance. He didn't know what it was either, but we had to get out of the house. Outside we crossed the street, supporting one another as it was impossible to keep a sense of balance while the ground trembled so violently. Unacquainted neighbors, dressed in nightclothes, gathered in front of their homes. A sense of helplessness was our common bond. Someone suggested that this was an earthquake. Looking back, I'm sure he was a native Californian. I thought of turning on the car radio since all power was dead. In doing so, the emergency station informed us that this was indeed a major earthquake of a high magnitude. When the movement subsided, we discovered that what had seemed like an hour was actually 90 seconds. The earth finally stood still, but the nightmare was not over.

In a short while, it was determined that the core of the quake was located near a dam only 7 miles from our neighborhood. In order to avoid the risk of the dam's collapse, we were advised to evacuate the area. I recall having one hour to collect some personal effects and proceed to a safe area. The evacuation itself was hasty, emotion filled, and very illuminating. It's interesting what's important to take when you have only one hour to collect your belongings. Kristen took her teddy bear and tape recorder; I took photo albums, personal papers, and Kristen--to start a new life.

As we drove from the rental home, we were made aware of the extensive damage that had been done. It was horrifying to see huge slabs of concrete and bricks lining the streets and freeways. Some of man's super structures, bridges, freeway ramps, etc. had been devastated in only a few moments. I remember wishing I could be sure there was a God during the helpless time when the earth moved. When it was safe to return home, sleep did not come easily. Aftershocks were nearly as frightening as the actual earthquake, perhaps more so, as we relived the fear each time the earth began to tremble. Aside from the physical property damage that had resulted, clinics were set up in the Los Angeles area specifically for problems related to coping with the quake. Fortunately, there were few deaths. This was attributed to the early morning hour of the mishap, but psychological problems, resulting in several divorces, one of which was mine, were later attributed to the quake. Surveys taken showed that the earthquake of 1971 had a profound effect on many lives, and that included Kristen's life. Later, she was to reflect on these effects in her lyrics.

Kristen, age 10

Chapter 3 - Interlude

As I said, my marriage to Kristen's father ended in divorce. Once that was settled, Kristen and I moved to Las Vegas to live with my brother Don and his wife Lynda. There, I enrolled Kristen in a day care and worked for an advertising agency. We only stayed there for a few months and then moved back to Buffalo, fueled by my brother's decision to rejoin our family business. It was in Las Vegas that I met the man who eventually became my second husband and adopted Kristen, Norm Pfaff.

I'll never forget the drive across the country. Don was in such a hurry to get back to the rest of his life, and I was not. Perhaps it was a sense of foreboding, but I never really wanted to leave the West. Little did we know what the future would hold.

Although I didn't find God in California or Las Vegas, He found me in Snyder, New York. Once in the Buffalo area, I moved upstairs from the Kearney family in Snyder, and I was their first tenant. They took a chance with me as I was unemployed and a single parent. But God knew what He was doing. It turns out they were a Christian family, and since I was seeking a relationship with God, I longed for the faith that they displayed. They became my friends and mentors. Kristen befriended their two daughters, and we had a grand time.

I got a job, enrolled Kristen in day care again, and I began a pilgrimage: a journey to establish a relationship with God that would take me over many mountains and through many valleys for some time to come. Within three years, I married Norm who relocated to Buffalo and adopted Kristen.

Kristen was self-motivated, pristine, very intelligent, witty, personable: a joy to all who came across her turbulent path. Whatever she set out to do, she did with great success and honor. School teachers were inspired by her, and her music teacher adored her. She grew up in Williamsville, New York, a suburb of Buffalo. Her childhood consisted of plenty of books, Brownies, and Girl Scouts. Her favorite toy was her tape recorder. She loved to record songs. She had an imaginary friend named Bobby Sherman who was a pop singer at the time. She was very close to family and friends.

For a writing class at Erie Community College, I wrote about Kristen's first day in kindergarten. I found taking her to school gave me mixed feelings. She seemed more prepared than I was. It was not easy for this emotional Italian mother to let go of her daughter. This is how I recall it:

The alarm rang. This was it! It was the first day of school and my little girl was leaving the nest. As I lay in bed procrastinating, my daughter Kristen peeked around the corner as perky and chipper as usual asking for breakfast. We stepped into the kitchen, where I fixed her what she wanted on this special day: pancakes, sausage and juice. I recall not being particularly hungry. Actually, I felt a bit nauseous. Who could eat at a time like this? Kristen could, of course. After breakfast, we started to get ready. While combing her lovely jet black hair, I looked at Kristen with pride. She was so lovely with her hazel eyes and fair skin. She looked like a china doll as we put on her new red plaid school dress. I looked Chinese as well with the slanted eyes I had from lack of sleep. I insisted on walking her to school despite her protests, refusing to let go until the last minute. I was hanging on until the bitter end. I knew Kristen would be all right when I tearfully waved good bye and she nonchalantly looked up as if to say, "Are you still here?"

Despite my feeling of pride and admiration for my daughter on her first day of school, I could not help but feel a sense of loss as I walked home alone. She was ready to go before I was ready to let her go. Perhaps if we, as parents, were made aware that it is normal to feel these mixed emotions, we would be better prepared for the beginning of many steps in setting our children free.

Kristen, 8 years old

As a creative 8 year old, my little girl continued to prefer her little tape recorder and microphone to any other toy, and to sing Girl Scout songs into the mic with her own embellished lyrics. Now, she began to study classical piano. The experience with her piano teacher is described in Kristen's journal, one of her many entries:

Childhood memory: 2/18/85

She [piano teacher] carefully rose to greet me at the door, wearing an outdated polka-dot dress and pinceney glasses. As I walked into her small, well-kept home, I sensed all the fragrances that made up her life: smells of fruit bread, cookies, furniture polish, and flowering plants, all with the stale, unwelcome stink of medication and old-age lying ominously underneath. Her living room was a museum of mementos, each revealing a special facet of her life, long and musical like a concerto: a white marble statue of Beethoven, photos of her husband and children in heavy silver frames, an untamed Mexican urn shouting bold fluorescent colors, knitted afghans in shades of beige and orange, and a threadbare rug that was once a sickly green, now deceased. The focal point of the room was a magnificent and regal grand piano, polished until it joyously reflected every nuance of its surroundings off its smooth mahogany surface.

I paid homage to that piano, her raspy and age-choked voice telling me to open my Bach. I willingly agreed, at once getting caught up in a surge of musical expression. My hands flowed effortlessly, yet timidly over the ivory keys until reality slapped me with a wrong note. My fingers trembled all over each other and fell, graceless to my lap. She never grew angry or impatient. With a soft chuckle, she commanded her gnarled, arthritic hands to come alive, and soon her twisted fingers were dancing across the keyboard, showing me, the apprentice, the correct fingering of the piece. Her flexibility was a rebellious stand against her aging: a defiance of the laws of nature, and a tribute to the fountain of youth that was music.

As I played on and on, she selflessly poured her knowledge and skill into me, and our communion was made complete. I passed beyond the limits of the average nine year old and reached that grey area where age does not matter anymore. Smiling and pleased with herself and me, she gave me a light kiss, her parched, lined skin, like sandpaper, on my little girl's cheek, and said good-bye.

(Later, Kristen submitted this entry as an essay in Sacred Heart Academy High School and received an "A").

Chapter 4 - Composition

A doctor told me that I was unable to conceive again, surprise! . . . . After a blessed and easy pregnancy, my son Jason was born on January 23, 1975. He was a delightful child, eight years Kristen's junior, and she loved having a little brother. Jason grew to adore Kristen, his big sister, and she loved it (most of the time). As she got older, though, she didn't appreciate her little brother getting into her things-- sibling rivalry in a normal, playful way.

Kristen with baby brother Jason

In 1975, Kristen's middle years were interrupted with a diagnosis of scoliosis. She wore a back brace for 2 years which was successful in straightening her spine. Again, here's Kristen's version from her journal:

February 7, 1975

I never thought that it would change my life--a crooked spine--so what? After all, I was only 8 years old; I never noticed the difference. My mom noticed it in the wedding, said I had bad posture and had to be checked out. The doctor said I had scoliosis. That's okay, I thought, I've read "Deenie", and I know what it's all about. Before I knew it, they were fitting me into this metal cage with devices and contraptions that tugged and pulled at my body. It felt weird, and I cried. Mommy said not to worry, it wouldn't last too long. The first day sitting and eating were impossible. I tried to watch "The Brady Bunch," but little steel bars were rudely cutting into my skin and the plastic corset was squeezing my guts out onto the floor. I cried again, but there was no choice. Putting it on was terrible, those little spikes that stuck in your thumb and drew red, red blood. When you are little, you are supposed to be free; I was in chains. I was in a prison. "No, I cannot play; I have to wear my brace for 20 hours now." I was older and I didn't want anyone to see it. "I am not an animal. I'm a human being wearing a big fat steel trap." I looked forward to the few hours of freedom I got. My mom's words echoed in my mind:"It won't last very long." I grew tired of hitting my head, getting in cars, and having to lean back in my seat to do homework. Once my bra unstrapped and I couldn't do anything about it because it was under a tee-shirt, under a brace, under a turtle neck shirt, under a sweater. As I grew older and got more time off, I began to depend on it. I wore it when I didn't have to; it was like a security blanket.

Oh no! I'm not growing up deformed; I'd rather go through any discomfort. I became very self-conscious. I wanted to grow my hair down to my waist to cover my abnormally grotesque back. I looked at the X-rays. Mom, is it really that bad? I feel like a sideshow in the circus--come see Kristen Pfaff, the amazing S-shaped woman. It's funny how people look at their lives in stages and plateaus--my life is in two classes: with the brace versus without the brace. Try telling a little girl she can't play outside in the snow because she has to wear the brace 20 hours a day (only 4 hours a day left); she can't pick flowers in the field (it's so hard to bend over); she can't even go to the bathroom (those clumsy little girl underwear that went up to the waistline would get under the brace), and then see how she turns out. I once blamed my mother for making me this way. She had spent one year in the hospital, getting straightened out. They say I'll never be straight though. My friends say it doesn't look that bad, but I know that's all that they see; at least, it's all that I see. I once said that I had half of an hourglass figure. It's true; I'd rather be straight as a poker than be half normal. Something has to always set me apart from everyone else. I remember playing the piano for 4 hours a day in the sweltering heat of summer, sweat crawling down my back, and collecting along the sides of the plastic bottom of the brace, and reeking when I took it off. I learned Beethoven's sonatas that summer. I never went to the beach. I guess having that brace gave me lots of time to develop different parts of myself that other kids weren't doing while they were out romping in the fields. It was much easier to lie flat on my back and read a book than to try to face a gaggle of screaming kids that were all thinking, "Why does she have on that ugly metal collar, and why does she look so fat? Hey, if we punch her, she won't even feel it. Ha ha." I remember Mike C. shooting rubber bands at our backs and laughing because we never felt it, but my brace protected me from knives and from being stabbed. I'm afraid, always was, but my brace covered me. Try to stab me and your knife will break, you villain! You can't catch me, I'm "the fiberglass man"; martial arts at its best, comes complete with bullet proof vest.

When Kristen was diagnosed with scoliosis and had numerous doctor appointments, I would reward her after each appointment with the latest issue of *Teen Beat*, her favorite magazine. (Years later, when I visited her in a Seattle Hospital with a diagnosis of cellulitis, I searched frantically for *Teen Beat*. Even though she was now 26 years old I thought it might make her feel better!

Later, I came across one of her journal entries discussing the term "monster" as it was presented in the Mary Shelley novel, *FRANKENSTEIN*. I suspect this writing referred to Kristen as she saw herself wearing her brace. Again she turned this writing into an essay which earned her another "A" in her English class.

Teenage Kristen

Kristen 1984: Who is the real monster?

The term "monster" is usually associated with both physical and spiritual characteristics. The creature is generally of a grotesque and deformed countenance, large in stature and frightening to behold. It is supposedly devoid of human emotions and morals, and performs malicious acts for no apparent reason, with no feelings of guilt or anxiety over these actions. In the novel Frankenstein by Mary Shelley, the definition is not so obvious. While Frankenstein's creation undoubtedly fits the physical criteria mentioned above, only Victor Frankenstein himself is spiritually disfigured. At times one wonders whether he indeed is human, or has he manifested inwardly what the monster portrays outwardly? In proving the ultimate innocence and goodness of the monster, it is important to not only examine his actions, but the motivation that prompted them, and also his feelings afterwards.

The creature was given life in an egotistical whim of Victor Frankenstein: his inane attempt to prove his supremacy over the rest of mankind by overstepping the boundaries of God. Victor felt that his creation would be a new and perfect specimen of life, that "a new species would bless me as its creator and source; many happy and

*excellent natures would owe their being to me."
However, when the creature is finally bestowed
with life, Victor flees into his chambers, unable to
acknowledge the hideous form as his creation.
Later that evening, the monster makes an attempt
at contact with his master, but Victor is overcome
with fear and leaves both his home and his
creation behind. Therefore, at the very onset of
his existence, the creature is abandoned and left
with no friend or companion to guide him. He is
forced to survive on his own.*

*Like a child, the monster absorbs the
sensations and actions of the people and things
around him. His learning process is purely trial
and error; by placing his hand on a burning log
he learns that fire is hot, by walking into the hut
of a stranger he learns that he is revolting and
appalling to man. It is this brutal realization that
has the greatest effect on the monster. He is
unable to be loved even by his own creator, and
he is also unacceptable in the eyes of others. The
creature laments, "Was I then a monster, a blot
upon the earth, from which all men fled, and
whom all men disowned?" His sorrow turns into
bitter hatred when, upon saving a young girl from
drowning, he is rewarded with "a miserable
wound which shattered the flesh and bone." The
monster becomes obsessed with the idea of*

punishing both mankind and Victor Frankenstein for the sins that have been committed against him. He vows, "from that moment I declared everlasting war against the species, and, more than all against him who had formed me." All of the injustice that was paid him in the past finally gains retribution when the monster meets William in the forest. Seizing the opportunity to avenge the creator that rejected him, the creature attacks the boy and places the blame on a close friend of the Frankenstein family, Justine. The monster's motives are clear; he has been deprived of a peaceful and happy life by the very person that has given him his existence; therefore, he must inflict pain upon Victor in return. The monster himself is merely a victim of the harsh circumstances of his early life and is essentially a good and just creature; however, his feelings of compassion and tenderness have been stunted in their growth and suppressed until almost nonexistent beneath his flaming rage.

Although the monster commits murder on several occasions, he does not do so because of a fiendish desire to destroy, and he does not take his offenses lightly. As he continues in his quest to avenge Victor, the monster is spurred on by "a frightful selfishness" but his "heart was poisoned with remorse." He is "heartbroken and overcome" by Clerval's murder, and as his revenge is finally consummated in Victor's death, the monster can no longer cope with the knowledge of the crimes he has committed and wishes death upon himself. Surely, this creature cannot be deemed an unfeeling brutal animal, but is merely a sensitive, mistreated individual that is groping desperately for his own identity, finding no suitable answers.

Victor, on the other hand, has always been sure of his identity. Victor sees himself as omnipotent: subject to no one but himself. He feels that he has been blessed with the gift of creation, and he exploits this knowledge in a selfish quest for superiority. He feels no guilt upon abandoning his creation, and once he begins to realize who is responsible for the murders of his family and friends, he does not attest to the fact that he is guilty due to the product of his laborious experiments. He is afraid that he will be blamed as the monster's creator; therefore, he remains silent and allows innocent people to be needlessly punished.

Victor's selfishness and cowardice are seen throughout the novel, as Victor disregards the dangers of the monster's vow to be with him on his wedding night and marries Elizabeth who is found dead shortly thereafter. Victor had made provisions for his own safety, but never gave a thought to the safety of his bride. Also, when given the opportunity to appease the creature by producing a female counterpart, Victor remains stubborn and egocentric and refuses to comply. As a result, another murder is committed. Victor's self-centered actions are not only detrimental to his forlorn creation but also bring harm to the people held dear to him. By consciously allowing his loved ones to be pointlessly executed, Victor becomes more of a monster than the creature itself.

Like the majority of the characters in Frankenstein, we are a people influenced greatly by outward appearance. Only by examining the intricacies of an individual's personality and mind can a logical conclusion be drawn. By delving deep into the darkened recesses of the warped mind of Victor Frankenstein, it is easy to see that although Normal in physical form, Victor is, by nature, a monster.

Kristen's bout with scoliosis took me back to my own struggle with the same medical condition. I spent ages 11 and 12 in the hospital for surgery and recovery in the crippled children's guild. Imagine going through puberty in plaster of Paris; it's no wonder my middle school years were less than joyful for me. I experienced death at an early age. Two of my ward mates died: one 12 year old of heart disease, and the other one of crippling muscular dystrophy at age 7. I kept a diary given to me by my Aunt Katy and Uncle Nick on Easter Sunday, April 1, 1956. My first entry read, "April 4, 1956: Today I came to the hospital. I was scheduled for surgery on April 11." As a result, I was not able to make another entry until the 19th. I wrote on the 19th that I was still having difficulty and needed help to eat. On April 24th, I was transferred by ambulance to the Crippled Children's Guild where I remained until October 22, 1957.

My special job at the guild was entertaining the troops. When a nurse took one patient to wash her hair, I would, in my plaster of Paris cast, roll over on the hospital cart and push myself around the room with my feet to visit the other patients. They got a charge out of that. By adding humor into this situation, I was able to get through my prolonged hospital stay.

I have so many stories about this experience that it could comprise another book. I can say that the good news during this time period was the birth of my baby brother, Terry, on May 2, 1956. I didn't get to meet him right away, but my mom and dad did bring him to the hospital with my younger brother Don (3 years my junior).

After I left the Guild, I didn't come home to normalcy because my mother and family overprotected me. But my greatest childhood memory, aside from the birth of my two brothers, Terry and Don, was when I visited my grandmother every Sunday during the school year and every summer in Lockport, where I was born. Those times restored a normalcy to my life.

Those were my experiences with scoliosis, so I had an understanding of what my sweet, innocent daughter was going through. I wanted so much to protect her and give her support because a mother doesn't want her child to suffer or feel pain. But they do, and they must as part of their development. Let me continue with Kristen's early years.

St Gregory the Great, 1980-1981
Kristen is 4th row, 4th picture

Kristen won a scholarship to Sacred Heart Academy in Buffalo, where she became a cheerleader and played cello in the high school orchestra. She became so good that she was asked to perform her own concert. Friends, schoolmates, fans of all ages made up her first audience. The concert began in high school, where Kristen's tiny, dainty figure was nearly consumed by the grandiose cello she played so beautifully in the orchestra. The contrasting picture of delicacy with the overgrown instrument strikes a chord of mockery in my mind and heart as I think of her being swallowed up by the musical fame she would experience one day as bass guitarist for Courtney Love's band, *Hole*.

During Kristen's senior year, Norm and I broke up, and Kristen began to change. I thought it was just the college life around the corner, but something else was happening, and it could have been precipitated by the breakup of my second marriage. She took an apartment in the city of Buffalo and started wearing a lot of black and partying quite a bit. Around that time, Kristen wrote this entry in her journal.

March 18, 1985

Conversation with the ocean: I was awakened one morning from a deep and peaceful sleep by a loud rhythmic, thunderous roar. The scent of salt and seaweed permeated my small bedroom and every now and then a seagull's high-pitched wail intervened. I was astonished to awaken and find the ocean perched magnificently and stately at the foot of my bed.

33

"Good morning little one" boomed the ocean. "I have often seen you gazing into my eyes, making plans, dreaming dreams for the future. I feel that we've got a lot in common, and I'd like to talk with you."

Needless to say, I was surprised to be graced with a visit from such an ominous and powerful being, and I replied, "How did you happen to notice me from all the millions of people that visit your shores?"

"There's a quality of energy and vitality in you that I haven't seen in many other people. Also, I think that, like me, you are outwardly active; always moving and searching for new and exciting experiences, but inside there is more going on that no one ever realizes. There are parts of you that have been touched by no other human being. Just like me, there are parts of me that are virtually unexplored."

"Yes, that's true," I replied, "but I don't consider that detachment a very good quality."

"Well, I think that you should try to open yourself up to others; you touch other people's lives, but like my fickle and temperamental tide, you quickly withdraw deep into yourself. Like my sometimes friendly, sometimes deadly waters, you

are also capable of holding and comforting others, but yet you can be demanding and cruel."

I was beginning to get offended. It's not often that one is criticized and analyzed by one of the awesome forces of nature, at such an unearthly hour.

"Hey look," I retorted, "I didn't invite you to come in here and list my faults at 5 A.M. There must be something about me that you admire."

"Don't be defensive, Kristen, it is not often that I travel so far to pay a visit to a human being. I'd like to thank you, for I sense that you truly appreciate my beauty. All of you artists are alike: writers, painters, photographers. You all have the ability to draw beauty from something that other people may find simple, or that they take for granted. Keep up the good work. You are only just beginning, but if you keep looking at me, at the sunset, and also deep into yourself, I think you'll find the happiness and aesthetic perfection that you have been searching for."

I was flattered and amazed that such a wise and omnipotent entity could see reason to call me an artist, but before I could voice my thanks, the ocean began to recede and all that I heard was this faint and warm message:

"Keep looking up, never cast your eyes downward, for there is more glory in the routine of daily life than you realize, and remember, if you ever need guidance, I will always be there to help you. Plunge deep into my waters, take the chance, and you will be rewarded."

Was this a premonition? After all, Kristen became a free spirit who thought she was invincible in the ocean of life.

Cheerleader for Sacred Heart Academy
and St Joseph Collegiate Institute

Chapter 5 - Aubade

During Kristen's senior year, she won a scholarship. She chose to attend Boston College and was scheduled to leave in September. I thought she would be all right, but in September, when we took her to school, I felt more than empty nest syndrome. I don't think she ever really came home the same person again.

Once at Boston College, Kristen took an apartment off campus with a bunch of girls, wishing to separate from the cramped quarters of the dorm. Change was happening, but her grades were excellent. She met a guy she liked a lot and brought him home to meet me. I wasn't impressed. He was strikingly handsome, but had a dark side that my sensitive spirit couldn't miss. Kristen secretly married him and took him to Nijmegen, Holland, where she was studying abroad as part of her English Studies program at Boston College.

She didn't tell me about this marriage. I found out from one of her roommates and was extremely hurt and upset about not sharing in such an important part of her life. Kristen did eventually tell me and sent me letters from Holland, telling me all about what was happening in her life. They also display her wonderful sense of humor. Here is one of those letters:

Letter from Kristen September 2, 1987

Dear Mom,

Despite the tears and strain, I'm really glad we got everything out in the open finally. It wasn't an easy secret for me to keep, and believe me I'm not proud that I kept it a secret. I made a decision which has changed and will continue to change my life, and I couldn't or rather didn't share it with anyone important to me. Blame my idiocy for deciding that I couldn't share it. During our first few phone calls on the subject, I felt that perhaps I could convince you that I was

38

confident in my decision--that maybe you would even come to Boston. Later, it seemed hopeless.

All of my life, I've been relatively quiet. I've followed the "program", and enjoyed it-- graduated from high school with honors, moved on to a good university and was successful. I've worked hard and plan to continue. Everyone in the family is proud of me for this, but how many real decisions have I had to make? Most times I simply went along with what "should" be done. When I started expressing some sort of individuality in dress and lifestyle, it was labeled weird, unattractive and rebellious. No one understood me. I felt alienated from all but my closest family who remained faithful, supportive. I came to one of the most serious major moves of my life and everyone got scared. Growing up too fast or something.

I know you don't doubt my judgment which is why I listened to what you had to say. Stubbornly, I remained firm in what I wanted to do, but I didn't want to hurt you at all. By not saying anything I took the easy way out and prolonged the pain I would cause the people I love so much. I took my life into my own hands and selfishly ended up depriving my family of what I would imagine to be a big dream. I am so sorry for this, honestly, but I am not sorry for marrying. It's so much better than when we were living together in so many ways, mostly, because I feel the commitment and promise in every minute of the day. Little fights are less apt to become big and complicated. If we start bitching about stupid things now, we just laugh and carry on with the major business of the day--keeping our heads above water in a very foreign country. Everyone we've met since we got here is introduced to us as a team--it's already tightened up our relationship. It's neat to be so young?? and so free and yet so serious and strongly together. We're both settled down and wild at the same time--no time for boredom. We are best friends first, and we play together as you probably noticed. After that comes the intimate part, and it's wonderful. I feel very lucky.

Christopher said he talked to his mother and you asked her: "So when are we going to visit them?" That made me so happy you wouldn't believe it. It seemed like before I even talked to you, you were on your way to accepting it somehow. Thank you for being so loving and forgiving. I never wanted to hurt anyone--I love my family very, very much. Even if it was bad judgment, I hated feeling like I couldn't tell

*anyone. What a bind I put myself in by being
dishonest.*

*I hope you can forgive me and even be happy
for me. I can't say much more, so let me tell you
about our experiences so far.--Amsterdam was
fun and crazy a real city with real city hours and
real city prices! The architecture is so amazing
there; everything is tall and narrow. The
cobblestone streets and canals remind me of a
clean Venice--it's incredible. We found a youth
hotel which was very reasonable: the "Adam and
Eva." With the 16.75 guilder (Dutch money)
charge came a traditional Dutch breakfast every
morning--3 pieces of bread, Gouda cheese,
salami, and hard boiled eggs. Most days, after
eating this sumptuous meal, we'd roam the streets
and go into little pubs for pints of Heineken, the
cheapest beer in Holland. Check it out in Buffalo;
I'm sure it's expensive. Our tolerance has
increased about 100% already! Nights we found
clubs that played something close to "our kind"
of music, or just roamed around the red light
district, where the hookers stand in the windows
of their place of business and try to seduce men
off the streets. It's funny at first, but it gets rather
slimy.*

Besides breakfast, our weekly fare consisted of ham & "kaas" (cheese) sandwiches ("broodjes" in Dutch), hamburgers, French fries, and little Indonesian rice balls called "nassi," which you can buy in dispensers in "automatieks" all over the city. The automatiek is like a self-serve McDonald's except with Dutch and Indonesian specialties. It's like those hospital snack bars where you can get a turkey sandwich by putting six quarters in the slot. These yellow-signed snack bars are a common sight, even in Nijmegen, and when you visit, I'm sure we'll take you out to one. The foods I've mentioned are the cheapest available--forget sit-down restaurants: 1. they're ridiculously expensive, and 2. they speak Dutch.

Supermarkets are strange here as well (everything is!). There are hardly any extras like what you'd see at Wegmans or Bells. Supermarkets are small and sell only food and paper products. For health and beauty stuff, you have to go to an "apotheek" or pharmacy. So far I've seen ONE brand of deodorant, TWO brands of shampoo, NO conditioner, and only O.B. tampons (yuck!). It's quite a switch from the aisles and aisles of goo at CVS or Pete N' Larry's. Anyway, this is more of a pain in the ass than I'd expect it to be. When I return to "The

States" (it's never called America in Europe), I'm going on a midnight shopping spree. All stores, I mean EVERY ONE, close at 6:00 pm (18:00 VVR)! How crazy! No 7/11 or Store 24 here. Actually, I've moved to a description of Nijmegen from a description of Amsterdam. At least Amsterdam stayed open late. In Nijmegen, if the buildings could be collapsed and folded and put way for the night, they would be. We arrived in Nijmegen at around 7:00 on a Sunday evening and felt like characters in a Twilight Zone special--cruising the dead streets looking for a "telefoon" booth. Plus we stand out like albinos in Harlem here. They dress safely and conservatively. We look dark, foreign, and even threatening here. It's obvious. But we've spotted a few different looking people and are waiting to discover the place where the rest of them are hiding out so we can meet them all and become instant celebrities! ☺ We have a great apartment for entertaining, just no one to entertain just yet!

When we first saw the place, I must admit was a disappointment. We seem to live in one of the only buildings in Holland built in the 1970's! You know, that generic, ugly type of building with light brick exterior! But inside it's nice and quite spacious for two of us. The previous owner left a lot of his own posters and décor behind--we took all that down and put our own stuff up 'cuz it felt like we were living in someone else's house!

This letter is already too long and rambling, but there's so much more to tell! I'll be brief...

Cigarettes- Everyone rolls their own cigarettes here because packs cost f 4.25 at the least! Talk about a strong cigarette! But the tobacco we bought is lighter than most, so even without a filter it's not too bad. It's gonna be hard to get used to rolling papers, though.

School- It's going to be pretty easy, I think. I have the advantage of being a native English speaker so I can read the novels faster and have a firm grasp on what's going on. On the other hand, the students here are much better educated and speak 3-5 languages fluently! So they have the mental edge and probably a lot of discipline.

Jobs- Looks like dishwashing for the both of us until we learn enough Dutch to get by! Yuck! The director of the program here said he'll see what he can do to get us hired somewhere. Without his help it'd be impossible.

TV- 6 channels: 3 Dutch, 2 German, and 1 Belgian. TV is boring here and we can't understand it anyway.

Language- Most everyone speaks English, but it's still hard. If you see a sign on a bathroom or in a store window, you can't figure out what it says. It's very annoying. Also, when you call someone on the phone, the person speaks in Dutch and has trouble understanding what you want right away. It's such a thrill to hear my language spoken well by someone other than Christopher. Imagine--he's the only person I've spoken to at length in 2 weeks almost! If he wasn't here...I'd lose my mind!

Bikes- I've never seen so many in my life! You see a bar, and if there are 100 bikes outside, it's normal. Hardly any cars, just bikes, bikes, bikes! I have one left from the girl that was here last year.

Okay, I'll shut up for now. The little things I've sent you are just samples of what I see in everyday life here. The wrapper with the flower on it was from a Dutch dessert bread, the bag is licorice (they have 500 brands here, all black!), the yellow one is regular wheat bread, and the silver wrap that says "jong belegen" is from 1 slice of Gouda cheese. That's all that is available except in expensive specialty delis. The map was given to me at the train station in Nijmegen, and I've written some things of interest on it. The little bag contained postcards and I thought it was cute. When I have money to spend, I'll send you some real things. I hope this is ok for now.

I love you and miss you very much! Please let Dad and Grandma and Grandpa read this letter too if you want since I can't write letters this detailed or I'd lose my mind and hand as well! Also, if you wouldn't mind sending those boxes as soon as you can--it's cold enough here already for winter clothes and jackets!!! You don't have to worry about the quilt and typewriter just yet. Thanks so much, PLEASE write soon, I'm starved of communication, and my mailbox is big and empty. Pass the word--I WANT MY MAIL!!

Love you so much Mommy (and Daddy and Grandma and Grandpa)!, I hope you know.

Kristen

P.S.- No, I didn't forget the coolest brother on earth! He has a separate letter coming.

P.S. - Can you PLEASE, PLEASE, PLEASE send me some "Nudit Crème Bleach for the Face?" They don't do that here I guess! I may give in and let my armpit hair grow, but I will not look like this the whole time I'm here! It's gross!

Unfortunately, Kristen's marriage ended in divorce six months later. I was involved in the divorce, but not the wedding!

Chapter 6 - Cadence

Upon returning to Buffalo in the late 1980's, Kristen took a job in a local hospital before enrolling in the University of Minnesota (U of M), where she had learned of their excellent Women's Studies program and English department. This time I thought she was on track and was putting a value on her education. She was such a good student. It seemed to come easy for her to get good grades.

Then in 1990, while attending the U of M, she observed many situations affecting student rights, specifically issues with campus safety, such as lighting and student communication. As a result of her concerns, she participated in a group, voicing its opinions to administration regarding improvement in campus lighting and other student issues. This involvement led to her counseling rape victims, as well as participating at the college radio station, Radio K.

She communicated with me frequently and was happy and loved Minnesota: the big sky and the wonderful people. It was there that the alternative music scene was so big and happening. She taught herself to play bass guitar and got together with Joachim (Joe) Breuer and Matt Ensminger to form a band called *Janitor Joe*. They were very popular and were signed by a record label called Amphetamine Reptile Records. I hated the name of the label and told Kristen so, but she only pooh-poohed the idea of drugs being related in the title. I was so naïve about it. I trusted her and didn't entertain the idea of drug use. Maybe it was denial. The other guys in *Janitor Joe* were awesome, and I really liked them. Although I didn't like the music, I appreciated their enthusiasm and talent.

Janitor Joe

I visited her in Minnesota and was not too impressed with her appearance. She seemed tired and overworked. Kristen always worked, and she was fiercely independent. When *Janitor Joe* was assigned a U.S. tour, they borrowed $1,000 from me for an old van (they paid me back faithfully every month for 10 months), and that van took them to their first gig in Toronto. Jason, who was then 18, and I attended the venue there, and I have to admit it was fun seeing her perform, even if it was located in a shabby part of Toronto. It was at this point when Kristen returned to Minnesota that she decided to drop out of the university and devote all of her time to music. I was skeptical, but she was 25 years old, and I had really lost control or veto power long ago.

Kristen with *Janitor Joe*

Her label got them a tour to California, and it was there that they met Eric Erlandson, guitarist for the band *Hole*. He loved her performance and since they were looking for a bassist at the time, Kristen was asked to consider doing an album with the band. Eric then wined and dined her and convinced her to make the move, although it was not an easy decision for her to make.

She was attached to *Janitor Joe* and didn't want to forsake them, but the opportunity to be on the Geffen record label with Kurt Cobain's wife was a pretty tempting chance in the music industry, and she couldn't pass it up. I'll never forget *Janitor Joe* at my home in Williamsville when Kristen was agonizing over the decision. I almost thought she had given up the notion, but after a little bit, she decided to accept. This was to be the beginning of the end of her life.

The next time I saw her was in July 1993 when my friend Liz and I were in London to see Kristen perform with *Hole* at the Phoenix Festival--a huge outdoor music festival in the suburb of beautiful Stratford-upon-Avon, Shakespeare's home.

Kristen

I observed that Kristen was frail and working too hard, sweating, and the guitar riffs seemed to overwhelm her. I stood backstage and cried for the entire performance, disappointed that I couldn't spend more time with her due to photo shoots, press conferences, etc. The whole experience was over my head and surely hers as well. When I returned to Buffalo, she was heading to Atlanta to record the album *Live Through This*, which would go on to sell over a million copies and went platinum in the summer of 1994. After many phone calls from Kristen in Atlanta, complaining about the schedule, Courtney's absences from rehearsals, and general unhappiness, I once again asked Kristen to leave the whole music scene. Opportunity or not, it was not bringing her any peace.

In February 1994, the album was finished and Kristen was bored. There was no work, she was waiting for the album to be released, and she was very antsy. She wasn't getting along with anyone in the group and was very unhappy. She didn't want to come back to Buffalo and thought of it as quitting or giving up. Around this same time, I received a phone call from Eric Erlandson that Kristen was very ill. He admitted it was due to an adverse reaction to drugs, specifically heroin. I was on the next plane to Seattle to visit her in a local hospital and found her hooked up to an IV, her arm badly swollen with cellulitis. All I can say is that she was not herself. One minute she wanted me there;

the next, she was throwing me out of the room. It was the longest five days of my life. I had taken time out from my job at the family business, had no money, stayed in a hotel, and had to rely on Eric to drive me around in Kristen's little car that my dad had bought for her. I was distraught. It was horrible.

I wanted to drag her home, kicking and screaming, but did not have the wherewithal to do so. She insisted on going to Los Angeles for an MTV photo-shoot right from hospital. (I wanted to go with her to make sure she was ok, but being the cute little girl that she was, she said "Oh mom, you don't take your mother to an MTV photo shoot." There was nothing I could do to stop the mad progression of events that would follow.

She did agree to move back to Minneapolis to reconnect with friends, her support group, and to participate in an outpatient rehab. At this point, she was contemplating leaving the band *Hole* altogether, which made me very happy. When I returned home from Seattle, I wrote this letter to Kristen, dated March 1, 1994:

Dear Kristen,

You have been in my mind and heart ever since I saw you in Seattle. I'm very concerned about you and the effect of this group and career.

I hope it's not just the money because you really haven't seen much evidence of that. If you have financial insecurity, you know that I will always do what I can. Terry was right there for us wasn't he? Please know that I love you and I want to trust you, but it's the world and its influence that I don't trust. You seem to have a strong support group in Minnesota and that is good. Just know that you are loved. You are always beating yourself up to excel in everything. Just because you thought you had to be an over achiever to be loved, doesn't mean it's true.

Love,

Mom

In April 1994, the news of Kurt Cobain's death was reported. It was at that point that I begged Kristen to come home. She was in Minnesota in an outpatient rehab program and was convinced she could handle this problem on her own. Meantime, I looked into rehab centers from Seattle to New York, trying to find a place for her to recover. She wanted to go to Hazelden, which was $10,000 for 5 weeks. The only way I could possibly get that kind of money was to borrow from my parents, and she insisted that she did not want them to know about her problem. This was out of the question. My hands were tied. We communicated daily. Kurt's death was the turning point. Geffen insisted that the band members attend the funeral and flew Kristen to Seattle. I offered to go with her. Once again, she said "Oh mom, you don't take your mother to Kurt Cobain's funeral."

There was nothing I could do to stop the chain of events that would follow.

When I didn't hear from her for a few days, I knew that she had used again even though the doctor in Seattle told her that if she did it again, she could die. She did it anyway; the drug had that much of a hold on her. Once again, I felt sick and helpless.

In May 1994, only a month after Kurt's death, *Janitor Joe*, still together, without Kristen, was going to Europe for one last hurrah tour, and they invited Kristen to join them. She had promised not to return to Seattle and had instead returned to Minneapolis for support. She continued counseling, and all of the possessions that she had remaining in Seattle were to be picked up by my cousin Mike, who was living in Iowa at the time. I had sent him and his wife train tickets, and they were going to get Kristen's things before the trip to Europe with *Janitor Joe* was planned. My first question was:

"Kristen, are you sure you are up to this physically, and in every other way?"

To which she replied that it's a chance to be with people who love her and experience places in Europe that she had not visited, and "Please trust me, Mom; it will be good for me."

"All right, then come right home after the tour," was my response. "Kristen, better yet, meet me in Minneapolis after the tour."

I got a plane ticket. Now it's Kristen's 27th birthday, May 26, so I have a beautiful card, but she's in Europe calling me from all of these wonderful places that she wants me to see one day, sounding so happy, cheerful, healthy, and drug free.

I'm actually relieved for her and the decision to stay with them for the duration of the tour but not to fly back to Seattle. She insists this will be okay.

"What about your cousin Mike picking up your stuff?" I asked. "He'll understand; I'll call him," she told me.

So it went. She was determined that she could make these decisions for herself, in spite of my efforts.

***

(The following newspaper column was published one week before Kristen's 27th birthday, and one month before her last day, June 15, 1994.)

"A *Hole* Different Thing: Kristen Pfaff lives through the U of M, *Janitor Joe* and *Hole*". *The Nightly*, May 19, 1994 - By Simon-Peter Groebner

From the basement to MTV in less than two years, one former University student has rocketed through more changes than most musicians experience in a lifetime. Kristen Pfaff is one quarter of Hole, *the celebrated Seattle-based rock band that released the highly anticipated album* Live Through This *last month.*

Pfaff may be best known as the bassist and vocalist in Hole*'s "Miss World" video; she's also "the dark-haired one" standing in the background in magazine photos of bandleader Courtney Love. But the music that Pfaff has been a part of is too often overshadowed by Love's notoriety and marriage to Kurt Cobain, whose tragic suicide coincided with the album's release a month ago. In a perfect world,* Hole *would be on top of it.* Live Through This *is at once a beautiful, explosive and harrowing record - soaring far above the band's 1991 debut* Pretty on the Inside. *Yet success has its sour side.*

On the first anniversary of her enlistment in Hole, *Kristen Pfaff reflects on her experience of near-stardom with a newfound wisdom. "I was so naïve," she says. "I wouldn't trade any of it for anything, because I know a lot more now than I did a year ago. I know a lot about the business and what it does to people." She softens. "I mean, Kurt is a primary example. He broke my heart, you know?"*

In the wake of the tragedy, Hole members have put the band on the long-term back burner, and Pfaff is back to being a Minneapolis resident. Sitting in her modest south Minneapolis bedroom, the 26-year old musician seems well-read and intelligent, humorous, free-spirited and genuine. It's very hard to imagine that she also has a hit record climbing the charts. "Yeah, apparently." She shrugs. "I feel really removed from it. I mean, you have no idea how removed I feel." She laughs oddly. "I have to pinch myself and remind myself that this is a part of me."

Outside the spotlight of the media circus, Pfaff has her own stories. Even before she began playing in subversive punk rock bands, she was provoking change. After transferring from Boston College to the U in 1989, she majored in English and then crossed over to the Humanities department during its heyday. As an activist with University Young Women and the Progressive Student Organization, Pfaff helped organize a raid of President Nils Hasselmo's office in *response to the rise of sexual assaults on campus. "We planned this secret thing and we all converged upon Hasselmo's office and stormed in--well, I missed this part. I was late for the takeover of his office, so I had to break through the police line to get in!" She laughs. "I was late because I was a teaching assistant--I was grading papers!"*

The demonstration did result in a task force on reducing sexual violence in the area and the 24-hour campus security we know today. Later, Pfaff served as assistant general manager to WMMR, Coffman Memorial Union's cable-only student radio station, which was the precursor for Radio K. She was part of the brainstorm that resulted in a student takeover of KUOM three years later. But by 1991, Pfaff felt that her time at the U had run its course, so she left. After accumulating 150 credits, she found herself too far away from a degree. "I graduated myself," she explains. "I just decided to start a band and forget about school."

With that goal in mind, Pfaff discovered her recurring knack for falling in with some of the most groundbreaking musicians around. Her first project, Drool, featured members of underground noisemakers the Cows and the God Bullies but *never got out of the basement. Coincidentally enough, the first incarnation of* Hole *dropped by a* Drool *basement party during its Minneapolis stop on the* Pretty on the Inside *tour.*

Next, Pfaff joined forces with guitar innovator Joachim (Joe) Breuer (of late-80's Minneapolis punk-noise unit the Bastards*) and together the pair formed Janitor Joe. In just one year, Janitor Joe quickly built up a local reputation, and prestigious Amphetamine Reptile Records released its debut album* Big Metal Birds *in March of 1993. "That whole period was really absolutely, just so exciting," says Pfaff. "I just felt like we could do anything."*

Big Metal Birds was hardly out of the gate, though, before Pfaff was suddenly swept into the world of Hole. Hole guitarist Eric Erlandson spotted Pfaff at a Janitor Joe gig in L.A. and told her that they were in need of a temporary bass player. "I just said I would go but I had no intention of joining the band whatsoever," says Pfaff. "I was expecting to learn a new crop of songs in the vein of Pretty on the Inside*, which was all I'd known of Hole. I think* Pretty on the Inside *was the same sort of 'balls-out,' angry record I had already made. So I didn't think I'd be intrigued or challenged by the Hole stuff. And* *when I got to Seattle, I was. I just really enjoyed learning and helping write the new songs and felt after that first practice in Seattle, 'Shit, I have a decision coming on, and it's gonna be a bad one. And a hard one.'"*

Her choice to sign on permanently with Hole *was respected on both sides. (*Janitor Joe *forged on with a new bassist, and the band's new album,* Lucky*, is due out June 1.) The amazing new music that would become* Live Through This *helped expand Pfaff's talents. "Hole, right now, we're essentially a pop band," she explains. "You know, it's a whole different thing. I had to learn a different style of bass playing, and while it may surfacely appear to be easier, it's harder. Because of subtleties."*

Pfaff still keeps a lot invested in her first major band, however. "I get my little BMI checks from Janitor Joe. Last time it was 242 radio plays--I got $19. It was the most valuable $19 I had ever gotten. And I guess I need to think about why that $19 means more to me than what I get from Hole*, you know. I think it's about that ownership thing."*

Nevertheless, Live Through This *is the greatest musical accomplishment thus far for all four Hole members--but even that silver lining has a cloud.*

The larger-than-life music world has offered Hole its share of downsides. The band has had to deal with poorly written and frivolous articles in Creem *and other rock rags, grueling 12-hour photo sessions, and the undying stigma of being pigeonholed "girl band," even though Hole has one male member. And of course, Courtney Love's every move is scrutinized by the tabloids.*

"There's a really sad thing that happens when business enters into music," says Pfaff. "It's something that I've always struggled with. And as long as it doesn't compromise the music right now, it's okay. But I'm really having a great time doing the things I'm doing now here: Getting back to friends playing music together, which I really missed."

Pfaff returned to Minneapolis, in part, to re-establish her home base in a brighter, more supportive musical community. "I couldn't get going in Seattle because the local scene was so stagnant. There's a lot more going on in Minneapolis." Currently, Pfaff is embarking on a short, one-time reunion tour in Europe with Janitor Joe. Meanwhile, she's back to collaborating: An as-yet-untitled, but very promising project with Hang Ups/Muskellunge *guitar wizard John Crozier is in the works.*

Hole plans to pick up its aborted tour plans in September. With luck, the future will treat the band more fairly, and Hole will receive the respect that Live Through This *warrants. Pfaff sees the prospect of her own potential fame as a necessary challenge. "The only thing I can say is I need to try and see what it's like. I can't anticipate it until I try it."*

In the meantime, Kristen Pfaff is leading a relatively ordinary life while her band continues to rise. "The life that this has taken on is just too much for me to even understand already," she continues. "When I have friends coming up and saying 'I saw you on TV,' or 'I saw you in this magazine,' it's just really unbelievable. And I hope it's not about being jaded; I hope it's more about not having it be a priority in my life. At the same time though I have to be aware of what an accomplishment this is. Because it is, you know? And I just can't be so nonchalant about it; there's a lot of bands that are struggling. And I gotta look and say I'm lucky in a way."

She reconsiders. "But I'll feel luckier when I'm onstage playing our songs."

***

In June 1994, my mother was admitted to Millard Fillmore Gates Circle Hospital with severe arthritic pain. After a trip to the grocery store, I returned home, and there were cars in my driveway which was unusual in the middle of the week. As I walked up the driveway, my brother Don came out to meet me.

"Mom?" I asked.

"No. Kristen," he said.

"Plane crash?" I asked.

"No. Drugs."

I fell to the ground in disbelief. Kristen had been found in her apartment the day before she was to leave Seattle. They said it was an accidental overdose--an accident. My brother tried to console me and urged me to go into the house. Everything faded. The most important thing was to bring her home--away from Seattle. Kristen's friend, Paul Erickson, later drove her U-Haul back from Seattle to bring all her belongings back.

Chapter 7 - The Other Side of Fame

Following her death, articles appeared in Seattle, Minneapolis, and Buffalo. A few listed her positive accomplishments while others, along with radio, television, and internet, referred to her as a heroin addict. I was angry about their insensitivity. The following are some of the more positive articles written about Kristen:

Kristen Pfaff: 1967-1994

When the news hit that Kristen Pfaff was found dead Thursday morning in Seattle of an apparent heroin overdose, a large portion of the Minneapolis music community mourned the loss of a remarkable human being. Pfaff was widely known as a songwriter and bassist with the Seattle band Hole (and on its powerful new album Live Through This), but she had made her presence felt here as a four-year Minneapolis resident. From her days as an activist for women's rights and other issues at the University of Minnesota to her involvement on the local rock scene, Pfaff was known to many as a positive force--undeniably bright, talented, and genuine.

Having interviewed Pfaff at length only weeks ago, it's clear to this writer that Pfaff was anything but depressed, self-destructive, or nihilistic. The speculation that she intended to take her life seems unlikely; she was in the process of replanting herself in Minneapolis after her first year with Hole, using the band's hiatus to lie low, enjoy herself, and play music with friends. She had grown cynical of the music industry and wary of the downsides of success (as epitomized by the case of her friend Kurt Cobain). But she also felt a strong sense of purpose to follow her musical fortunes. She was fiercely proud of her accomplishments and felt the drive to continue.

Pfaff was possessed of an inspiring aura--she was free-spirited, intelligent, funny, and, frankly, beautiful--all which had an undeniable effect on those around her. "I wouldn't be [playing music] if it wasn't for her," assures Joe Breuer, with whom she formed Janitor Joe, her first major band. "And I think it was definitely for the good because that's really what I wanted to do."

We're left with the troubling question of Pfaff's apparent drug use--especially with the *combined losses of Stephanie Sargent (7 Year Bitch), Andrew Wood (Mother Love Bone), Cobain (whose heroin use may or may not be implicated in his suicide), and others, both in and out of the music scene. By all accounts (including her own), Pfaff was getting away from the drug culture; this may even have fueled her decision to live apart from the rest of Hole in Seattle. But somehow, on a short visit there to move her possessions home, she fell victim. The fact remains that heroin continues its restored popularity among musicians of Seattle, Minneapolis and elsewhere.*

Pfaff's death may wind up playing in the media as "just another senseless rock 'n' roll casualty." For members of Pfaff's world, it was instead the latest case of unfair misfortune for a good and virtuous person. If Kristen Pfaff is to remain provocative as in her life, she might awaken us to the urgency of turning this trend around, and stripping some of the allure away from heroin and IV-drug use. Finally, we can always remember her magnetic persona--and her equally impressive art.

Simon-Peter Groebner

Some Last Notes on Kristen Pfaff

On a warm night last June, Kristen Pfaff sat down to write in her daily journal. It had been a tumultuous year for the 27-year old musician from Amherst who was living in Seattle.

Pfaff had dedicated her life to rock music and was on the threshold of stardom with the band Hole. Despite that achievement, she carried some heavy burdens. She longed to get back to Minneapolis, where she had attended college and was part of a vibrant music scene.

She hated Seattle. It was there that she had experimented with drugs. It was there that Kurt Cobain, husband of Hole's lead singer, Courtney Love, had been plagued by heroin and rock stardom and killed himself.

Pfaff had been to Seattle for nearly a year, but left in March 1994. She returned in April for Cobain's funeral. In June, she went back a final time to get her belongings.

Earlier, she told a reporter from the University of Minnesota newspaper what she had told the members of Hole: "Look, if you want me to be happy and sane, I just need to get back home."

Home was on her mind as Pfaff sat in her apartment on June 11 and wrote in her journal. Outside, her U-Haul trailer was packed for a trip to the Midwest. On this night, however, Pfaff was thinking about more than music or record sales or a cross country drive; she was dedicating herself to survival. "I'll write it on my sleeve," she would say in her journal, "I know how to live."

Five days later, Pfaff was dead.

Seattle authorities listed the probable cause of death as "acute opiate intoxication," due to heroin.

Until now, Janet Pfaff, Kristen's mother, has not commented on her daughter's death. "There has been enough printed about her death," said Mrs. Pfaff, who lives in Amherst. "I want the focus to be on her life."

Her daughter will be inducted into the Buffalo Music Hall of Fame at the Buffalo Music Awards ceremony on Oct. 19 in Blind Mellons.

"Kristen was a star, not in some media sick way but in a way that I felt gratitude for knowing her," Love wrote to Mrs. Pfaff. "She was impressionable and extremely sensitive to her surroundings; she was also intensely pragmatic,

which was why I didn't worry that much (about her). Kristen was like an oak tree, so strong but so frail."

Norm Pfaff, Kristen's father who lives in Denver, said he was proud of his daughter; he also called her "the kind of kid who could do anything she set her mind to do."

Sometimes, such talent and expectations exact a heavy toll. "My sister faced the burden of overwhelming potential," said Jason Pfaff, 19.

Mrs. Pfaff is gratified at Kristen's Hall of Fame induction and wants people to know her daughter was an intelligent and talented woman. Kristen won a scholarship to Sacred Heart Academy, where she was an honor student. She also earned a scholarship to Boston College and was an honor student there and at the University of Minnesota.

In Minnesota, Pfaff became consumed by the new movement in rock music. She taught herself to play bass guitar and hit her stride playing in a loud and cutting-edge band, Janitor Joe.

Janitor Joe signed a deal with Amphetamine Reptile Records. Early in 1993, Janitor Joe played a gig in Los Angeles, and Eric Erlandson, guitar player for Hole, was in the crowd.

Erlandson was impressed by Pfaff's style and invited her to join Hole for a weeklong tour in Europe.

Hole was an aggressive, tight band with pop overtones and Pfaff's bass made the group that much better. Geffen Records promised to give the band's new album, <u>Live Through This,</u> a major push, but Cobain killed himself four days before the album was released. Such turmoil and tragedy was just part of a year in Seattle that changed Pfaff.

"I was so naïve...I know a lot more now...about the (music) business and what it does to people," she told the Minnesota Daily a month after Cobain's death. "I mean, Kurt is the primary example. He broke my heart, you know."

Mrs. Pfaff remembers that period. "After Kurt committed suicide, Kristen and I talked every day by phone," she said. "She was devastated by his death. I asked her please to come back home, to get out of Seattle."

Mrs. Pfaff had rushed to Seattle in February over what she labeled an "incident" that hospitalized Kristen. The mother stresses her daughter was not a regular drug user or addict.

"In this brief time in her life, for the first time, Kristen had a fling with drugs." Mrs. Pfaff said. *"I think it was peer pressure. I think it was part of a music scene in Seattle where drug use is glamorized and emphasized."*

"What bothers me so much is the way this has been sensationalized about Kristen. All this happened in the last year of her life. She did have problems in the last year, but what about her other 26 years? The media missed the fact of what an accomplished musician she was, what a good person she was, and all the good things she did."

In May, Kristen Pfaff went on a brief tour of Europe with Janitor Joe. Friends say she enjoyed playing with her old band and was happy. The tour ended in early June.

"She was in good spirits, and I'll never understand why this happened," Mrs. Pfaff says, sitting in her kitchen. Outside, it's a cloudy fall afternoon with a chill in the air. Mrs. Pfaff walks out to the back patio, where she has planted a garden in honor of her late daughter. It is in full bloom with yellow and crimson flowers.

"It's the first time I ever planted anything like this, and I'm amazed it turned out so well," she says with a smile.

There have been few smiles for Mrs. Pfaff in the past three months. One of the hardest moments came when Kristen's U-Haul arrived shortly after her funeral.

"We had to unpack it," Mrs. Pfaff said. "I had to take out the pillows and my daughter's teddy bear and everything else she packed. It was very hard."

Mrs. Pfaff hopes her speaking out will help others. "I guess I'd tell kids to be careful, try to make wise choices and trust God to supply all their needs, even when the world lets them down."

"I would tell parents to stay close to their children and teach them about love and forgiveness. I told Kristen to be careful; there are so many temptations out there. She told me, 'Mom, I can handle it.'"

Mrs. Pfaff doesn't blame music for the tragedy. "I don't want to blame rock 'n' roll for what happened to Kristen. This isn't just another story about a rock star who bites the dust on drugs."

"Kristen was not a wild kid. She was an honor student who cared about music and the world around her. She commanded respect. She was very proud, had a radiant personality and was brilliant. The way she died doesn't make sense to me, but her life was an inspiration to me and the people who knew her."

Jason Pfaff, who plays drums in a local band, Rainbow Girls, was one of those inspired by his sister. "Kristen was open-minded about music, even before she began playing in a band," he said.

"There was a lot more to her than music. She was an activist who wanted to change things in a positive way. When she joined Hole, it wasn't about fame or money; she did it because she believed in the music."

Kristen Pfaff's friends and associates offer similar accolades,

"Even in her weakest and lowest moments I saw a strength in Kristen that was so pure and undeniable," said Elizabeth Davis, Kristen's former roommate in Seattle. "I will always think of her as a strong woman."

"She was an inspiration to me...(with) her lust for life, her energy, her desire...Kristen was

not about drugs (but) unfortunately, she had people around her who did drugs and romanticized drugs...I think it was the only time she let herself be free of the discipline she imposed on herself. It is so (hard), being a strong woman."

Mrs. Pfaff is still trying to put everything that has happened in perspective. She is a devout Christian who says: "I know one day I will see my daughter again. If I didn't have that hope, I don't know what I would do."

And though her words are tinged with sadness, there is joy for Mrs. Pfaff when she thinks about Kristen. "I couldn't have asked for a more beautiful daughter in every way."

-Anthony Violanti

On June 20th, the day before Kristen's memorial service at the Metropolitan Chapel on North Forest Road in Amherst, NY, I gave Pastor Andrews a letter I had written to Kristen. Here's what I wrote:

75

Dearest Kristen,

I don't understand all of this. It has been said that God loans us our children for awhile, that they really don't belong to us. They are special gifts for us to love while we have them. I can thank God that I had an opportunity to love you for the short time you were here, and I believe you knew you were loved. A lot of people don't have the opportunity to explore their potential and develop their talents as you did. Many people don't have the privilege of doing what they love in following their dreams. I'm grateful you did have that chance and you will be deeply missed. I couldn't have asked for a more beautiful daughter in every way.

I love you.

Mom

The rudeness and interruptions from the uninvited parties detracted not only from the spiritual side of her death, but also the family's grieving.

After the funeral, I sent Pastor Andrews a letter thanking him for the memorial service and apologizing for the numerous news media and the rude paparazzi. I wrote:

Dear Pastor Andrews,

Thank you so much for your inspiring words and messages which brought the Bible to life. You definitely impacted the lives of many people with your ability to preach a sermon that had both meaning and wit and a very clever use of the language in order to reach audiences of all ages.

I know it was difficult for you to conduct the services for Kristen. You not only had a difficult time with the cause of death, but also with the climate which allowed it and the characters who appeared in your church, including Amherst police and Hole and Nirvana fans who were decked in corresponding T-shirts, etc.

Yet, you were able to add spirituality and love to a very difficult occasion.

Thank you.

Janet

Besides family and friends' support, I received many fan letters and emails. All helped me during the grieving process, not only right after her death but even up to the present. Here's an email from a fan:

Thank you so much for emailing me about your page. I took a look at it, and the sight brought me to tears. It is extraordinary. Kristen

77

has been a major influence on me for a long time, artistically as well as emotionally. And I will be happy to tell you that you're not the only one who shares these feelings for her. What happened to Kristen was a horrible, horrible thing, and it could have been prevented. But it also makes people aware of what is happening, and they think, 'My God, if something like that could happen to her, then it could happen to me too...or my sister...or friend...or father, etc. How many people have to die before we realize that the problem will not go away if we act like it doesn't exist?'

Thank you again for emailing me. Love forever, Leahbell.

***

Friends and family were very helpful. Jason and I spent a week in California visiting family in 1995, and later I was invited to visit friends in Tucson and Phoenix. I chose to travel on Amtrak so I could continue writing, and I thank God for that opportunity.

I received a message from a childhood friend of Kristen's who now teaches at a high school in Phoenix. Imagine that...right where I was headed. Who knows what God has in mind. I am open.

***

On the train last night, somewhere over central or southern Illinois, during miles and miles of sunset, as I traveled back in time 2 hours, the sun was setting amidst the vast cornfields and soybean plants. All I could see were fields, a large sky, open country--all beautiful to behold. I woke up this morning in Texarkana, Texas, headed for San Antonio. This life and loving God and the opportunities that He gives me are helping me cope.

***

Laura Joplin, Janis Joplin's sister, had written a book about Janis entitled, *Love*, which helped her with the grieving process. After reading it, I realized that she and I both shared a similar sense of loss. As part of her book, she described her reaction to hearing of her sister's death:

I became furious at those faceless rock-and-roll people who had considered themselves Janis's friends. How could they let her do heroin? Everyone was doing drugs, including me, but heroin was different! Didn't anyone care enough to intervene? I chastised myself for not having been a better sister and knowing about the heroin. Why didn't somebody do something?

Laura quoted a passage from *Love* concerning her mom's way of locking her feelings in an internal closet that held all the warm memories of an adored first child. Laura's mom, Dorothy East, had written this in response to a fan's letter:

How do I cope with the memories? Simply by remembering with joy the happy times and the many, many times of laughter we had.

How do I cope with remembering the problems? Trying to do so without bitterness, knowing my children were loaned to me; they were not my possessions.

How do I cope with bitterness? I just give it up without reservation and without looking back wondering "if this" or "if that." To fail to do so will result in a warped perspective which twists upon itself. It is not easy; I try and keep on trying.

How do I cope with the anguish of losing a daughter? Simply by being grateful for the time with her and the riches it did bring, and NEVER, NEVER forgetting.

How do I forgive? It takes working at. It MUST be done. After all, I am NOT the judge of any person, either evil or good. The religious thesis in prayer is, "Forgive My sins as I forgive others." That being so, I must do it.

This helped me as one mom to another over the loss of a child. Thank you, Laura Joplin, for making me realize that, like you, by letting go of my grief, I will be free to love again. By holding on to the grief as though it's the last thing I had of my daughter, it's a silent resistance to accepting her death. My book will release my grief. Thank you, Dorothy East, for reminding me of forgiveness. As mothers who have lost a child, we belong to that special club that we didn't sign up for, and would never choose.

I have read books by other mothers about going through the process of grieving. One book in particular was, *Beyond Grief: A Guide for Recovering from the Death of a Loved One*, by Carol Staudacher. She wrote:

You cannot get through grief unless you experience it. If you hide it, deny it, or dull it, it will only be prolonged. Your emotional pain must be lived through in order for it to be lessened, and gradually eliminated.

As far as I'm concerned, not a living soul can know how I feel and what it has been to **live through this,** and no one has the right to even suggest how I should be doing or what I should be feeling. Today's dead end may be necessary for tomorrow's breakthrough.

**

Later, I donated some of Kristen's writings to the archives in the Rock and Roll Hall of Fame in Cleveland, Ohio.

Janet in front of Cleveland
Rock & Roll Hall of Fame

Chapter 8 - Free Fugue

In 1996, I entered into pastoral counseling with Pastor David Drake from the Metropolitan Chapel on North Forest Road in East Amherst, New York. In addition, I decided to find out more about substance abuse that led me to a secular counselor. She, Marcy Brimo-Walle suggested I read *The Artist Way*, by Julia Cameron, which discussed journaling as a way of healing. I bought the book and accompanying journal and began my years of journaling. She recommended that I write in the morning faithfully for three months and then after that time, I would reread what I had written. Both counselors helped me greatly, and I will always remember them and their guidance.

Three months later, I began to reread my journal, highlighting some entries and making remarks in the margins. After a while, I realized that the highlighted entries and notes referred to young people--from kids to young adults. Such entries included: "I need to say this to kids"; "I've got to talk to kids"; "Kids need to hear this."

Where was God in all this? Finally, there was God. I had found my mission--to dignify Kristen's memory and help others. This realization inspired me to develop my message that I should share with kids, teens, young adults, and even parents.

My message wasn't just a warning about drugs, but that faith in God can be a source of strength and provide a safe place to go in times of crisis. I had made my decision: I didn't need to be a great artist or writer. Instead, I needed to be a tool for the master artist to deliver the message.

Here are some excerpts from my journal.

Thursday, June 13, 1996: Day 1 of morning pages. 3 a.m., kind of early. I guess I had it in my head to awaken early, so here I am. I'm not quite sure how to fill the pages--could be depressing since I am in the process of grieving. The anniversary of Kristen's death is coming up...It's the juggling...that has me in this state of mind. Had a good counseling session. This journal and the book are the result of a session in counselor's office. She drew 3 circles; one was labeled "facts", the second was "my interpretation of the facts", and the third circle was labeled "future." The counselor said I have a choice of accepting the facts in the first circle and not remaining in the second circle, questioning why and to what purpose, or facing the third circle. So I decided to face the future as an adventure, like all my life has been. I so need to know what the message is. Not clear to me yet. I was told writing would be cathartic. I'll probably get down to the mundane daily business soon enough, but it is kind of refreshing to write some of what led up to this for now. Daily meandering is not meant to be art, but it is art because it is an expression of feelings, thoughts, and struggles. How can that not be art? What is art if not an unveiling of inner thought, or ideas and expression, revealing in some form such as writing? There is so much inside of me. I have reserved many thoughts, ideas, dreams, feelings. I have been so frustrated in the past. I have had so many disappointments as a result of not being able to share with anyone for any length of time. Now I have a chance to express the innermost me without fear of judgment. I find that exciting.

6/14/96: It was in 1971. I had returned to Buffalo with Kristen who was 4 years old to fulfill my desire to get to know who God was after experiencing the earthquake of '71 in Los Angeles. I was led to return home and God used my brother and Lynda to get me back. I resisted because I loved California in spite of earthquakes. They chose to leave and, having no

85

other family out west besides Aunt Jean, who had her own problems, I had to come back home with them. I found an apartment that I felt secure in and moved in above the Kearney's on Hamilton in Snyder, NY, a nice neighborhood to raise a child. I was experiencing good changes and spiritual evolution. Norm was calling from Las Vegas. I sensed he wanted some of this, too, for himself. He ended up moving to Buffalo and we became engaged. That was quite a time in my life--many changes and much excitement. A sense of security I had never known, and the chance to fulfill the desire to marry before Kristen went to kindergarten so she could have a nuclear family like everyone else. Good intentions--not necessarily enough reason to marry, which would later unfortunately end in divorce.

6/15/96: On artist dates…. I used to have artist's dates all the time without labeling them as such. Treks to the country, exploring little towns, talking to strangers. I miss the freedom in doing that…I've never liked long term goals. I've always been short term--part time…. "Hi there! Gotta go now!" Never want to stay anywhere. I want a t-shirt that says, "You don't get it--you just don't get it." I may have to have an artist's date right now. The silence is deafening. The unringing phone is brutal. I hate everything today and everyone. I also hate my hair--so there. Now I've admitted my neurosis.

6/16/96: They say love of money is the root of all evil. I think people's attitudes are the root of all evil. It's the attitude about money, not money itself that is evil. They say, "Say no to drugs." I say, "Yes to positive choices." Now to find the positive choices is the key. What are they? Do they involve money? Do they involve attitude?

Monday, 6/17/96: My garden is full of bouquets of deep crimson flowers. It is awesome. How wrong it is to judge people.... This seems particularly jumbled today--scattered thoughts is the weather report. Occasional sunshine, some clouds, every now and then, a shower of tears. The weather of my heart--the storms of life have taken a toll there. The people in my life who are in the dark concern me. I wish to send out love today to them.

6/19/96: I love the early morning before the bullshit starts. It's so peaceful and fresh with so much potential, like a newborn baby. A bundle of potential. Journaling is good. The problem as I see it with journalism, i.e. the media, is that they are so anxious to get to the facts that they miss the feelings. I wrote a letter to the editor of Rolling Stone *when Courtney did an interview that wasn't favorable to my daughter. In the letter, I asked where the sensitivity was for the families and friends of people in the news who lost their lives to drugs. What about the positive side and contributions of these people's lives? Doesn't that deserve notoriety? Only the tragic part gets published--the good news is small mention to the media. However, the letter was not published.*

6/20/96: Kristen's biological father used to delight in putting me down. His own insecurity came across as a superiority complex, and being naïve I bought into the oppression and became intimidated, unable to open my mouth to give an opinion at all. In 1970, I had the opportunity to verbally forgive him and share my spiritual development. He was so moved that he wanted to reconcile. In a sense there was a reconciliation of attitude. He was a very intelligent man, far ahead of himself in many ways like his daughter. She reminded me of him, and sometimes it bothered me.

I have had a block in my piano playing concerning chording. I always wanted to understand it but didn't give it enough effort. I am tired of just being able to read the music and being limited to the arrangements of others. Also true in my life it seems. Kristen's dad could play by ear and so does Jason, my son. I have an original piece of music that I have copyrighted and recorded (early 80's? –Mercyhurst College). Even though my piano teacher told me I had talent, I didn't believe her. I thought anyone could learn if they put their mind to it. Besides, it was just reading other people's music.

6/24/96: Fifty-two years ago, I was born in Lockport to parents who were separated by WWII. My dad didn't even see me until I was two. I bonded with my maternal grandmother in his place. She was so dear to me. Her name was Liberata, meaning freedom, much like the word libretto, small book. I used to call her "Ma." She was so good. Mom and I lived with her for a while, until my father returned from the Philippines and New Guinea where he was stationed. Mom told me about what an adjustment it was for them coming back together after two years of letter writing and pictures. She said she didn't even know him when he got off the train. To me, it seemed very romantic and I always sought that kind of romance in my life. I was a happy child until I was diagnosed with scoliosis at the age of 11. I spent almost a year in the hospital and went through puberty in Plaster of Paris (much like what Kristen endured). A painful surgery and seeing other children die were part of that experience. It made me extremely sensitive and acquainted with death at a young age. Not without a sense of humor through it all. I got through a difficult time, but with scars inside and out. After that, I was pampered and protected by parents as a natural reaction to an unnatural situation (again, I did the same for Kristen, although she fought me--wanted to be independent and not show how much all that bothered her). I remember thinking I was so open minded once. Then, the challenge comes.

6/25/96: It looks pretty outside. Everything is so green and the flower garden is so beautiful – deep crimson and purple with the occasional white pansy poking through. These images inspired me to write the essay, "The Garden of My Mind":

What shall I plant today? Seeds of love, hope and joy, or negatives from the outside--weeds of doubt, confusion, mistrust, anger. Don't have to really plant these weeds; they keep coming up anyhow. So I have to weed and feed, use Miracle Grow, *and, as roots of these weeds are pulled, it hurts, then afterwards it is beautiful again. Until those dumb weeds come back, that is. Unless the root is taken out, the weed will keep coming back.*

Sometimes the weed is disguised as a flower or future flower, so we nurture it and water it along with the good stuff, but it has the potential of choking the life out of the healthy foliage if we leave it in the garden too long. There are some weeds that spread like ground cover and look so pretty until they wrap themselves around a healthy plant and snuff it out. Does God see us this way? I hope he takes those weeds and turns them into flowers because I cannot bear the thought of anything just dying without purpose. To change form and become in the transition, a beautiful flower is more comforting, loving, and easier to accept. We are blessed with many varieties of flowers in life--some more colorful than others, but each with something to offer the whole garden.

Just like the flowers in my garden, some have to be gently moved, others can survive when plucked and moved in a more crude fashion. Some survive better in the shade, others in the sun. The more frail the flower, the more tender nurturing is needed. Some flowers seem to weather the storms better. Kristen's experimentation with life had no boundaries--she had a lot of opportunities and experiences that the average person does not have in a lifetime. She was able to explore her talents and creativity, and unfortunately, she tried too many things that were no good for her. She thought she was invincible, and yet she was frail, but the most beautiful flower in my garden.

As you can see, I have been richly blessed by so many varieties of flowers in my life, colorful personalities. Kristen was the most precious flower of all.

I read somewhere:

After a while, you learn that even sunshine burns you if you get too much, so you plant your own garden, and you decorate your own soil instead of waiting for someone to bring you flowers, and you learn that you really can endure; that you really are strong; and you really do have worth; and you learn, with every good-bye, you learn (Anonymous).

With every good-bye, you learn. That's putting it mildly, my darling daughter. Bringing you into the world was the easy part, letting you go, saying good-bye, unbearable.

In one of Kristen's writings, she echoed some of my thoughts:

Sometimes the sky darkens and fills with odd shapes and threatening clouds and the buildings that once made a city a home appear alien and imposing.

And sometimes, when all you want is for your world to keep spinning on the same steady axis, it suddenly stops and leaves you rooted to a spot where you don't particularly want to stand.

The storm can cry for your cold, angry tears or you can cry with it and let it wash and soothe and equalize, and you always have a choice with a grief that is as stubborn and unmoving as this house or this city or this earth.

Soon you will find that you can move.

You can wave your fist at the blackness and bleakness and scream at the sterile concrete which surrounds you.

And when your world finds its rhythm once again, what you will see is hope.

And looking over your shoulder, you may see love and realize that it has subsequently sheltered you the whole time.

There is nothing I can say to help walk you through this, but I can walk beside you, walk ahead when you need to, and I will always be here, loving you the best way I know how--quietly and completely.

6/26/96: I am blocked in music. I think that will be an area to overcome. I've also been blocked in other areas of work. I don't always get it. I need a t-shirt that says, "I don't get it," on the front and, "You just don't get it," on the back. We don't always get it. Life is like a lighter: sometimes you have five or six of them, and other times you have to use the stove.

Karen called me a "steel magnolia" today. That was nice. I'm not sure how true, but a compliment for sure. I'm learning to say no. What a lesson. I like what Karen said about being filled to overflowing. To first be satisfied where you are at. Then God brings someone in to overfill so that when someone is taken away, it won't be so devastating. (Note from the editor: I think this is a scary concept!! So when I feel full and someone else comes into my life, should I be afraid that I am about to lose someone else?!?). To be filled with the Spirit, as opposed to what is out there – not much. Full of joy, peace, understanding, love, compassion, fortitude, insight, tenderness, forgiveness, praise, meekness, humility, soft-spokenness, kindness, empathy, trust, positivity versus negativity, sorrow, hate, distrust, bitterness, anger, emptiness. The only way to come close to this goal is through the Spirit of God. Surrendering all of the negatives to be replaced with the new ingredients that edify, comfort, and soothe. This is the mission and it is not impossible. There is some unresolved conflict over the circumstances surrounding her death. I am committing it to God at this very moment today. I give it to God, 6/26/96. Two years later. Two years to wonder, deliberate, hesitate, deny, cry, grieve; be angry, hurt, disappointed, embarrassed, humiliated, jilted, deprived, robbed. I release these emotions today. I let go of all of it! Amen! I forgive those who do not know what they have done, including Courtney, Eric, Patty (members of Hole), and those dark people in Seattle. Deal with them, God. You do it! Show them their ways. You are the only one who can. If you choose, you can use whatever instrument it takes.

While on a spiritual retreat to Stella Niagara Convent, Lewiston, NY, near Niagara Falls, I was made aware of a labyrinth, a sacred place, on the grounds. A labyrinth is one of the oldest contemplative tools known to humanity, used for centuries for prayer, as well as personal and spiritual growth. It offers only one route to the center and back out again. A labyrinth is an approach that gently and faultlessly leads a person to the center, regardless of the many twists and turns negotiated in the process. By walking the Stella Niagara labyrinth, a person rediscovers a long forgotten tradition of being reborn spiritually, and it can help a person remember that his or her life is a spiritual journey by setting foot once again on his or her own path.

Although there is no "right way" to walk the labyrinth, there is a wrong way. As in life, when reaching the first hurdle, I wanted to jump over it to get to the next trail. I thought, "This can't be right." I'm sure there was something wrong. I was going my own way. This only led to more confusion, and I kept showing up on the outside looking in because I didn't have the patience to follow the path to the center the way it was designed.

So I kept thinking that people were watching me from the windows and noticed my confusion. But who cares--I'll try it again, this time following the path exactly the way it went. I did not try jumping over the hurdles, desperately trying to get through them. Instead, I analyzed why they were placed there, and I miraculously got to the center by going around them. In my humanness, I tried to get over the hurdles and roadblocks but realized God wouldn't allow me to go over them and instead guided me around them. He didn't allow me to plunge through the stumbling blocks, but allowed me more freedom by going around them while looking back to see where I came from or looking ahead to see what I had in front of me. Just an easy path to follow to the cross.

Stella Niagara's labyrinth is a Christian pattern, an equally armed cross, visible in a rosette, a six-petal design representing a rose, the traditional symbol for the Virgin Mary. This experience helped me get back to my Christian path and, ultimately, in touch with God. It contributed to the process of grieving and letting go of negative thoughts.

Finally, I could see a pattern created through the journal and reinforced by everything else that touched me as I went through the grieving process. I would take my message to kids, teens, young adults, and parents. Kristen, an intelligent, talented, beautiful soul, had given me a reason to share the story with the hopes that someone would be helped, and perhaps choose not to take the last "hit," or even better, the first one.

Chapter 9 - Animato

Kristen's ten-year high school reunion was in June of 1995 and her classmates honored her with a collage of photos that I helped put together and a keyboard with her name engraved on it for the music department. I wrote a letter to the students of that class from my pain:

"I don't know what happened that night in June, 1994, but she was on the way out of a lifestyle that did not agree with her. We had many conversations prior to June 15th, and she was finding her way back to her faith in God. She was not depressed; it was not a suicide. I can only believe this was a terrible accident."

***

In his book titled, *When Grief Breaks Your Heart*, James Moore states that when someone you love dies, the best way to express your love for your loved one is to pass on his or her influence, take up and live your loved one's best qualities, because this will keep their memory alive. That is what my mission became, and I realized that it was not impossible to do this. Mother Teresa once said, "I know God said He will not give me more than I can handle, but I just wish He didn't trust me so much." I felt those words to ring true for me.

I kept asking myself what I could do now that I realized there was a pattern behind messages in my journal. Then, one day in 1996, there was a blurb in the Eastern Hills Wesleyan Bulletin: "Do you care about teens? Would you like to help some teenagers?" *Would I?* I responded.

As a result, I spoke to the youth pastor of Eastern Hills Wesleyan Church who informed me of a Back-to-School Bash featuring an alternative band named *Painted by Moses*. Church members' kids were encouraged to invite their unchurched friends. *What a platform for my message!*

When the youth pastor asked me to speak at the concert, I gathered my notes, my journal message, my story, pictures of my precious, beautiful daughter, and a copy of the platinum *Live Through This* album, sent to me by David Geffen Productions. That was my material.

I arrived unsure of myself. It was my first time speaking about Kristen. Trembling and terrified, I walked to the microphone. A lot of kids had turned out, and they were all looking at me, waiting to hear what I had to say. "I am standing before you, not because of any great faith or spirituality on my part, but because I have experienced a great loss in my life. This is not the reason I would have chosen to speak to you, but the one I have been given."

And then I proceeded to tell them the story of how a young, beautiful, and talented girl had her life cut short in such a tragic way. I shared the way God was helping me through the loss and the fact that my faith had been challenged in a tremendous way. I shared the scripture *"I will never leave you nor forsake you"* (from the 27th Psalm). And I told the story of how Kristen was the bass guitarist in a famous alternative band and proceeded to share how she died of an accidental overdose, and how this last image of her was not what defined her. My mission was to share from a mother's grieving heart how none of us are invincible, and to share the dangers and temptations they would someday, perhaps, have to face.

I asked if any of them had heard of the group Hole, or Kurt Cobain. Wow, there it was, my bridge to kids. Had they ever! I had their undivided attention. I shared how common in our society it is to glamorize the use of alcohol and drugs. "I'm here to tell you there is nothing glamorous about it." I shared how the insidious drug heroin (formerly associated with back alleys, and slums) is now the cheapest, purist, and easiest drug to obtain. It is used among professionals and on college campuses everywhere.

When I spoke with the Seattle police on the occasion of Kristen's overdose, they referred to it as a "fad" in the 90's. A fad! They said they didn't have enough manpower to investigate the number of deaths and crime associated with heroin.

Neither the government nor the private sector has done enough to reduce demand for drugs, or get them out of our schools, neighborhoods, and our communities. Every day, the epidemic robs us of lives that would otherwise make a difference in this world.

Treatment is great, but prevention is even better. People who say that a drug-free society cannot be achieved have it all wrong. You can't achieve a cancer-free society either, but society doesn't tell the researchers to stop looking for ways to try. Billions of dollars are being spent on fighting the war on drugs to curb drug abuse, yet the government has not stopped the illegal flow of drugs because there is too much money in it.

Money should be invested in dealing with underlying problems that lead to drug abuse, parents should be alerted when their child is hospitalized or arrested for illegal drug use, and be educated about signs of drug abuse. Society needs to spend less time and money exploiting the sensationalism in the media and focus on the cure.

I didn't start out to preach about drugs, but I have been affected in a very personal way and have a choice of being bitter or better, pitiful or powerful, and I admit there are days when I am overwhelmed and have so many unanswered questions. It's at these times that God will miraculously use a kind word from a friend, an inspirational message, a song, or just some way to let me know that He is there for me. I know in my heart that I am not alone.

I shared with the students how difficult it must be as a teenager in these turbulent times, and I also talked about peer pressure (at any age). Kristen experienced peer pressure.

I ended my message with:

"There are few families that aren't touched by tragedies in some form. Your faith may not have been tested to the degree that mine has. But you will be challenged, or perhaps someone you know will be challenged. You will have a choice to turn towards God or away from Him. His divine justice permits that freedom. My hope is that if even one of you meets this challenge and draws closer to God, my mission will be accomplished through you. I leave you with this prayer, by Clarissa Estes:

Refuse to fall down. If you can't refuse to fall down, refuse to stay down. If you cannot refuse to stay down, lift your heart toward heaven and like a hungry beggar, ask that it be filled, and it will be filled. You may be pushed down, you may be kept from rising, but no one can keep you from lifting your heart to heaven. Only you.

"The one who believes 'nothing good can come from this' is not listening. Remember hope is grief's best music, and true hope can be found in God."

***

I don't know how I did it, but I got through the speech. After I left the front of the church, I nearly collapsed into my seat in my car and burst into tears. The emotion was overwhelming. Afterwards, kids came up to me, some crying, some curious. All anxious, some just to know if I had ever met Courtney Love and Kurt Cobain. There were some that were sincerely grieving the loss of a musician that they knew and loved, and some grieving their own personal losses. All this, and I had only just begun.

This was just the beginning of a series of speaking engagements that would take me to many places including the United Kingdom, allowing me the privilege of sharing my story and God's love with many kids and giving me the opportunity to tell people who my daughter really was, and what her accomplishments were. So many of her qualities had been missed by the media, the press; *Rolling Stone* magazine referring to her as merely another drugged-out musician. I was given a mission, a purpose, a reason besides the commonplace existence I had come to know. I now knew that God was in it, and this task became something I could not have done without His strength. I had become acquainted with grief in a way that would impact many people's lives.

***

Mission Team before trip to England

In July 2002, I had the opportunity to accompany a mission group to London, England, for ten days with Brad Ringer and twenty-one teenagers. In order to be able to go, I needed to seek out support to sponsor me. As a result of my sponsors' help, I was required to pay only $10 for the whole trip! While in England, we stayed with member families of the Birmingham Church and spoke to their school-aged children about the dangers of drugs and addiction. From London, our group traveled to Stratford-on-Avon and lived at the local mission. Our work consisted of gardening, house repairs, and other daily tasks like laundry, etc.

It was here that I had the opportunity to return to the site of the Phoenix Festival where I had seen Kristen perform with *Hole* in 1993. My purpose was to speak to a women's group about drugs and addiction, but with a slightly different spin than our presentation to the children.

***

I had been contacted by the "Partnership for a Drug Free America" and flown to New York for a meeting of thirty VIPs of this prestigious organization to speak about the loss of Kristen. There wasn't a dry eye at the table when I finished sharing the story. They told me that by personalizing my experience and showing them a mother's perspective, I had put a face on the efforts of their work, and they offered to give me some tapes to use in my mission to speak to kids.

A representative of the Oprah Winfrey show contacted me to appear on her show, but I wasn't' ready to tell the story on national television. The format was "parents in denial," and I needed to come to terms with a state of total reality. It was not the right time.

Every person must discover and stand in his/her own light, without judgment or condemnation. Then he/she can decide whether it is okay to walk away to protect his/herself from being pulled into darkness and wrongdoing. It is a choice of freedom, leaving chains behind. Remember, it is the individual who makes choices about drugs and decides whether or not to use them.

I'm not here to tell anyone to stop or just say no, but to **Stop and Think** of Kristen's life and my grief as a parent.

This message (and book) is a labor of love but **it isn't easy living through this**, and it is not supposed to be, I guess. Kristen's death has affected me deeply, so my goal is to preserve her memory in order for it to live on and, in doing so, bring meaning to the lives of others faced with drug decisions. This has been a challenge of my faith, and I don't want to turn anyone off, but I cannot leave out the promises of God, who said, "I will never leave you nor forsake you. I will be with you always." This has been a test of my faith. In The Bible, Paul said, "Nothing can separate us from the love of God who is in Jesus Christ, our Lord." God has gotten me this far through this turbulent time.

Jason and Kristen

My son, Jason, is a talented and gifted musician also. At the age of eight, he began playing piano with no training whatsoever. In many ways, I thought I would lose him when I lost Kristen because I was unable to encourage him in his music since it was so closely intertwined with Kristen's life. The day after the discovery of Kristen's body, I shared this with him on a rare occasion when we walked together. "Jason," I said, "I can't encourage you to pursue a career performing music on stage."

I am so glad that my initial fear was unwarranted. Jason has been through more than most people, and I think it has made him stronger. He has really developed himself spiritually, and we grow closer as time moves on. Jason is now building up his own music-based company and recording studio, and works on international soundtracks and independent films. He writes and has written in-depth about Kristen someday intending to complete an inspiring film about her. He knew Kristen in a different way than a parent could know. They were very close, and her death seriously impacted his life. "She steered me away from becoming more ignorant than I could have become," says Jason. "She opened my eyes and pointed out perceptual trends I was learning in school like how to be racist, fascist, and just an overall prick without a conscience."

The following lines include Jason's thoughts about his sister that he shared with me:

Kristen had open eyes but didn't live long enough to learn how to deal with it. When you leave your nest and go out into the world to see what's really going on, and get bombarded with ideas, trends, movements, and people that are pointing out all of the insane things that are really going on, it's totally overwhelming. The initial thought is that I have to fix this somehow. We don't know what our responsibility is or what's true, what's not, or what we should be doing about it. Kristen was the type of person who was going to do something about it, but the negative emotions bogged her down and self medicating, well, maybe was a rational thing at the time, to bring back at least an ounce of happiness like she once had growing up in a comfortable suburb with a loving family. She didn't live long enough to find the solutions to these issues, but the good news is they exist.

Lots of variations of spirituality and real educational movements are on the rise. It seems as if we really have no choice but to evolve at this point. Everything changes, and we can't stay the same way and keep things the same way; it's pointless, and everyone feels it, especially our youth. When they are in school, and nothing resonates, they wonder what the hell is wrong. They aren't into it because something within them knows they are not being properly educated. We all want to learn, but ideally things that are of real value.

Drugs and addiction are a hugely underexposed epidemic in this country, but drugs were never the issue, and I won't go there. People intoxicate to be happy, and to deal with emotions. Learning how to be happy is not taught in schools. Learning how to manage emotions and build real relationships with people is not taught in schools. Other things that are not taught in schools are things like addiction and addiction management, personal responsibility, spiritual tools, alternatives to using drugs, how to manage money which I might add is pretty important in a Capitalist driven world, and further how to become who you really are.

While we're at it, learning how to discover one's talents and abilities so that one may manifest a career path they actually enjoy partaking in, wouldn't hurt. We're looking at deep societal issues here. This is an adult world; take a look around. What does society provide for youth? Bowling alleys? There's nothing for kids to do. The creative people with the best ideas have no money to launch their projects, and a lot of them would probably come up with amazing things for children and society as a whole. Things are changing however. Consciousness is on the rise, and people are stepping up and creating a new world. Nothing will bring back my sister, and I can't be pissed at anybody about it; I can only look back and remember how lucky I was to be so close with her for the time I had with her. Time to evolve. Be grateful for the abundance you have in your life, and you will always have enough. Take more than you need, then you're in more treacherous waters. But there is a lot of hope, a lot of help, a lot of beauty. If you look for it, you will find it.

On a happy note, Jason became a father on February 15, 1997. The birth of my grandson, Luke, was a new beginning for me.

What a reward! A continuation of life, to fulfill my dreams, to carry on the family name, and to live through endless possibilities. I was called at 5 a.m. and got to the hospital at 6:30 a.m. At 1:33 p.m., Luke made his entry into the world. He was 7 pounds and 13 ounces, and 21.5 inches long. He had curly golden brown hair, long majestic fingers, and would prove to be intelligent (which was obvious from the start)--a little miracle. It was official--Grandmother status achieved! This bundle of hope and joy became my greatest honor.

***

I found myself in between Kristen's death and its grief, and my recovery. Specifically, the in-between or middle represented the progression or process of change. James Moore addresses the in-between stages of life in *When Grief Breaks Your Heart*: "Sometimes, to get to the end where we are going, we have to be willing to be in-between. It isn't fun being in-between, but it is necessary. It will not last forever, and it may seem like we are standing still, but we are not. We are standing at the in-between place. We are moving forward even when we're in-between." For the young teenager, these turbulent times are often comprised of feelings of expectancy and incomplete action rather than a leisurely process with music of its own. It is the in-between stage of not always realizing the harvest at the end that is so difficult and creates confusion.

If grieving is the dignity of being wounded, then I don't know how else to take what I've been through. I never thought of myself as artistic or creative or anything out of the ordinary, but my daughter's death has given me a purpose. I have learned sensitivity, although her death created more pain than usual. On the other hand, it allowed me to experience deeper joy. Now I'm learning about friendship on a newer plane where I don't give less, but I expect less and sometimes nothing at all. I'm getting hurt less, but there is definitely something missing in my life. This is why I found it easy to accept a relationship with God. Another side-effect of my grief was the difficulty I had seeing a mother and daughter, hand in hand, shopping or in church. I hurt because I was reminded of my relationship with Kristen and how we used to do the same activities.

I recall reading this spiritual message on a card at a funeral parlor years later which I came to incorporate into my speaking engagements as a beautiful way to view Kristen's death:

There is no death. I picture myself standing on the seashore. A ship at my side spreads her white sails to the morning breeze and starts for the blue ocean. She is an object of beauty and strength, and I stand and watch her until she is a speck of white cloud, just where the sea and sky come to mingle with each other. Her diminished size is in me, not in her, and just at that moment when someone at my side says, "There, she's gone. There are other eyes watching her coming, and other voices ready to take up the glad shout, Here she comes; here she comes." And that is dying.

In light of what I have just written, a fan named William wrote a letter addressed to Kristen after her death:

I didn't know you [Kristen] in life, but people who knew you said you were a sweet heart, an angel of some sort. The stars are right, the moon is beautifully lit, and you're smiling down from heaven. I know how it feels to lose someone close. It's hard; eventually we come to terms with it, not really getting over it, but being better because that's what everyone wants us to do. A great guitarist playing bass, you will always be missed by your friends, family, and me: one more person who didn't know you but became a fan.

The loss of my beautiful, creative daughter and her potential gifts has affected me in the deepest way. In my goal, to preserve her memory and bring meaning to other lives, I have decided to view her as not having died, but having graduated because God has a higher purpose for her and for me to help accomplish or fulfill this.

Again, from *Beyond Grief*, Carol Staudacher writes:

"You need to tell your story, not once, but repeatedly. The old phrase 'You need to get it off your chest' has a great deal of truth because you do feel heavier at heart."

***

In a book by Claudia Black, she wrote, "Surround yourself with people who respect and treat you well."

Her words gave me additional insight.

That's so good. What a great goal. That shall be my goal in 2010. Synchronicity. What is synchronicity? Webster defines it as, "To occur in time, arranged events for coexistence or coincidence simultaneously occurring at the same time." Am I trying to read "synchronicity" into the events of my life like astrology, or reading into things and trying to make it fit because we moms want so desperately to connect the dots and events in our lives and in turn be connected?

I have learned that my speaking engagements have contributed to the synchronicity in my life.

I've listed some of speaking engagements from September 1996 to March 2013 later in this book. It took me many years to realize that my speaking engagements are a ministry, not a soap box.

In one of my speaking engagements in March 2013, my audience consisted of home-schooled children, ranging from elementary to high school age. I was very nervous, as it was my first time delivering my message since 2006. I approached the podium with my binder of notes, and I began with the summary of Kristen's life, her love of music, and her involvement with the music industry, Courtney Love, and Kurt Cobain. I talked about *Live Through This* and showed the kids the platinum album and explained that Kristen was never able to see the fruition of her hard work. I concluded my talk with how far I have come since my daughter's death but indicated that it is still an ongoing process for me.

After I finished, I was overwhelmed with emotion. I had gotten through the whole thing. As I started packing up my materials, one girl approached me and told me that she had been clean for two days, and that my message had really gotten her attention. I could not believe it. Several more children came up to me and told me stories about friends or relatives who were going through the same struggles. I left the church feeling that I had accomplished my goal - dignifying Kristen's memory--by reaching at least one child.

Chapter 10 - Fine

Through the grieving process, I searched for a way to preserve Kristen's spirit along with the University of Minnesota Scholarship for the Arts. I was able to do so using speaking engagements.

In my journey through grief, I now understand what Ted Menten in his book, *After Goodbye,* meant when he wrote that some people in the labyrinth don't really want to find the exit because being lost and not being responsible is a comfort in itself. He adds that to find the exit would mean coming home again and with the responsibility of re-entering life, a life without a loved one. He goes on to write that by successfully traversing the labyrinth of grief, one can emerge on the far side and re-enter life, maybe never feeling whole again but healed.

There are many reasons why people use drugs that can eventually lead to addiction including pain, depression, excessive pressure to perform, and last, but not least, peer pressure, as I have highlighted in my message to kids.

And so, in my journey toward healing, I too have experienced addiction, denial, and fear of re-entering life. When all is said and done, it is better not to cry that it's over, but to smile that it ever happened and that she was ever here, even for a short time. Thus, my journal, along with my journey, are the words of my soul expressing the music of Kristen's soul. She was like a balloon without a pilot, free to go anywhere she pleased. She was a free spirit who thought she was invincible in the ocean of life. In her last journal entry, Kristen wrote, "I'll write it on my sleeve--I know how to live."

And now, nearly 20 years after her death, I'm still learning how to "live through this".

Early Achievements

Kristen was an excellent student, receiving awards in many areas, including:

Honor Roll, Saint Gregory the Great, 1980

Scholarship to Sacred Heart Academy, 1981

Merit Award: Funniest, 1985, Sacred Heart Academy

Merit Award: Most Dedicated, in Track and Field, 1985, Sacred Heart Academy

Certificate of Appreciation for *The Torch* as Features Editor, 1985, Sacred Heart Academy

Scholarship to Boston College, 1985

The Starfish!

One day a philosopher was walking along the beach when he noticed a figure in the distance.

Getting closer, he realized the figure was that of a young man picking something up and gently throwing it into the ocean. As he approached the philosopher asked, "Young man what are you doing?"

The young man replied, "Throwing starfish back into the ocean. The sun is up and the tide is going out. If I don't throw them in, they will die."

"But young man," the philosopher said, "Don't you realize there are miles and miles of beach and hundreds and hundreds of starfish? You can't possibly make a difference!"

After listening politely, the young man bent down, picked up another starfish and threw it into the inviting surf.

With an inspiring smile, the young man said to the philosopher

"I made a difference for that one!"

Adapted from original story by
Loren Eiseley (1907-1977)

Speaking Engagements

I have been invited to speak to a number of groups and at schools throughout the US. Here's a list of speaking engagements.

Date	Location	City
9/7/96	Eastern Hills Wesleyan Church	Clarence, NY
10/14/96	Channel 7-A.M. Buffalo- TV Interview	Buffalo, NY
10/15/96	Iroquois Central High School	Elma, NY
10/16/96	St. Mary's High School	Lancaster, NY
11/6/96	Nardin Academy	Buffalo, NY
11/13/96	Christian Central Academy	Williamsville, NY
3/14/97	Nardin Academy- Spiritual Wellness Week	Buffalo, NY
4/97	Victory Assembly Church- Telethon to raise money for anti-drug programs	Tucson, AZ
8/97	Kingdom Bound Music Festival	Darien Lake, NY

Date	Location	City
11/97	Freedom Village	Lakemont, NY
1/98	Sheraton Inn-Pure for God Rally	Buffalo, NY
4/98	University at Buffalo	Buffalo, NY
6/98	Renaissance House	West Seneca, NY
7/98	Partnership for a Drug Free America	New York, NY
11/98	Notre Dame High School	Batavia, NY
1/99	Musician Assistance Program	Los Angeles, CA
4/01	Amherst High School-Health classes	Amherst, NY
4/01	Kids Escaping Drugs Telethon	Buffalo, NY
2/02	Clarence High School	Clarence, NY
7/02	London, and Stratford-upon-Avon	England, U.K.
1/05	Partnership for Drug Free America	New York, NY
4/05	North Tonawanda High School- Spiritual Week	North Tonawanda, NY
4/06	North Tonawanda High School- Spiritual Week	North Tonawanda, NY
6/06	Vigil for Lost Promise-Drug Enforcement Agency	Washington, D.C.
3/5/13	Eastern Hills Wesleyan Church- Fuse Youth Group	Clarence, NY

Family Left Behind

Janet, Grandma, Uncle Terry, Uncle Don, Grandpa

Alex, Andy, Anthony, Matt, Chris, Ashley,
Katy, Brent, Kristen, Jason, Sarah

Uncle Don, Aunt Eileen, Aunt Carol, Uncle Terry,
Grandma, Grandpa

Aunt Jean, Janet, Jennifer, Sandy, Michelle

Luke   Jason and Gramma

Aunt Linda, cousins Andy and Sarah

Cousin Mike Esposito   Dad Norm Pfaff

Kristen and Cousin Debbie   Cousin Anthony

Club 27

My son, Jason, learned that there were many musicians who died drug related deaths at age 27, thus *Club 27*.

In order for this number not to have any superstitious value, I found comfort in the 27th Psalm of the Bible. I share these verses in my message to kids:

Vs. 1: The Lord is my light and my salvation - so why should I be afraid? The Lord protects me from danger - so why should I tremble?

Vs. 10: Even if my mother and father abandon me, the Lord will hold me close.

Vs. 14: Wait patiently for the Lord. Be brave and courageous . . . Yes, wait patiently for the Lord.

(Verses taken from the *Life Recovery Bible New Living Translations*, Tydale House Publishers, Inc. Wheaton, Illinois. 1998. Print.)

Members of Club 27

Kristen Pfaff (*Hole*)
Sean Patrick McCabe (*Ink & Dagger*)
Freaky Tah (*Lost Boyz*)
Kurt Cobain (*Nirvana*)
Fat Pat (*Screwed Up Click*)
Richey James Edwards (*Manic Street Preachers*)
Ron "PigPen" McKernan (*Grateful Dead*)
Wally Yohn (*Chase*)
Robert Johnson (Blues Musician)
Jesse Belvin (R&B Singer)
Dave Alexander (*The Stooges*)
Brian Jones (*The Rolling Stones*)
Pete Ham (*Badfinger*)
Chris Bell (*Big Star*)
Gary Thain (*Uriah Heep*)
Jimi Hendrix (Guitarist)
Janis Joplin (Singer)

Alexandre Levy (Composer)
Valentin Elizaide (Mexican Banda Singer)
Nat Jaffe (Jazz Pianist)
Louis Chauvin (Ragtime Musician)
Maria Serrano (*Passion Fruit*)
Jeremy Ward (*The Mars Volta*)
Arlester "Dyke" Christian (*Dyke & The Blazers*)
Helmut Kollen (*Tirumvirat*)
D. Boon (*Minutemen*)
Pete De Freitas (*Echo & the Bunnymen*)
Alan Wilson (*Canned Heat*)
Malcolm Hale (Spanky and Our Gang)
Jim Morrison (*The Doors*)
Roger Lee Duerhan (*Bloodstone*)
Mia Zapata (*The Gits*)
Amy Winehouse (Singer)

Musical Glossary

Animato — animated; to make alive

Aubade — morning or dawn music

Cadence — closing strains of a melody or harmonized movement

Composition — the broadest term for writing music, or for music so written, in any form for any instruments or voices.

Con Spirito — with spirit; lively

Fine — the end of a piece

Free Fugue — composition written with more or less disregard of strict rules.

Interlude	a piece of music, usually relatively short, (intermezzo) that is inserted
Libretto	"small book", the text to which an opera or oratorio is set
Overture	opening; a piece of music that serves as an introduction to a longer work
Prelude	an introductory performance, action, or event
Selah	a Hebrew word meaning "Stop and Listen". In music a selah is a rest; no music played in the rest, but the making of music in it.

Works Cited

Ammer, Christine. *Harpers Dictionary of Music.* 2nd ed. New York: Harper Collins Publishers, 1987. Print.

Baker, Theodore, et al. *Pocket Manual of Musical Terms,* 5th ed. London: Schirmer Trade Books, 2003. Print.

Cameron, Julie. *The Artist Way.* New York: Penquin Putnam, Inc., 1992. Print.

Groebner, Simon-Peter. "A Hole Different Thing: Kristen Pfaff Lives Through the U of M, Janitor Joe and Hole." *The Minnesota Nightly* 19 May 1994: NP. Print.

---. "Kristen Pfaff: 1967-1994." *The Minnesota Nightly* 27 June 1994: NP. Print.

Joplin, Laura. *Love.* New York: Villard Books, 1992. Print.

Menton, Ted. *After Goodbye: How to Begin Again After the Death of Someone You Love*. Philadelphia: Running Press, 1994. Print.

Moore, James. *When Grief Breaks Your Heart*. Nashville: Abington Press, 1995. Print.

Staudacheer, Carol. *Beyond Grief: A Guide for Recovering from the Death*. Oakland: New Harbinger Publications, 1987. Print.

Violante, Anthony. "Some Last Notes on Kristen Pfaff." *Gusto: Buffalo News*. 7 Oct. 1994: 22-23. Print.

Whitfield, Charles L. *Boundaries and Relationships: Knowing, Protecting and Enjoying the Self*. Deerfield Beach: Health Communications, Inc., 1993. Print.

Kristen's Monument

Kristen Pfaff   1967-1994

Kristen loved her extensive collection of 7" discs (45 rpm records). The number 7 influenced the design of her monument by her longtime friend Matt from Buffalo. The stone is designed in 7" increments; it is 7 feet tall, 35" wide, based on the shape of her favorite necklace.

Her monument is located in Forest Lawn Cemetery, Buffalo, NY.

More information on Kristen Pfaff is available at HonorKristenPfaff.com.

Some of Kristen's writings and awards can be found in the archives at the Cleveland, Ohio, Rock and Roll Hall of Fame and Museum (rockhall.com).

Information on Jason and his music is available at warmjetsmusic.com.

Selah

There's no music in the rest, but the making of music.

Stop and Listen

91306002R00076

Made in the USA
Columbia, SC
19 March 2018